The Man Who Loved Seagulls

Essential Life Lessons from the World's Greatest Wisdom Traditions

Osho

ST. MARTIN'S GRIFFIN ♒ NEW YORK

The material in this book is selected from various talks by
Osho given to a live audience. All of Osho's talks have been
published in full as books and are also available as original
audio recordings. Audio recordings and the complete text
archive can be found via the online OSHO Library at
www.osho.com.

www.stmartins.com

All scripture quotations are taken from the Holy Bible,
King James Version, Cambridge, 1769.

Book design by Jennifer Ann Daddio

Library of Congress Cataloging-in-Publication Data
Osho, 1931–1990.
    The man who loved seagulls : essential life lessons from the
world's greatest wisdom traditions / Osho.—1st ed.
        p. cm.
    ISBN-13: 978-0-312-38863-8
    ISBN-10: 0-312-38863-2
    1. Spirituality. I. Title
    BP605.R34M36 2009
    299'.93—dc22

                                            2008040695

First Edition: February 2009

10 9 8 7 6 5 4 3 2

Printed and bound in India by Replika Press Pvt. Ltd.

Contents

Preface

Aristotle has defined man as a rational being. Man is not rational; and it is good that he is not. Man is ninety-nine percent irrational; and it is good that he is because through irrationality all that is beautiful and lovely exists. Through reason, mathematics; through irreason, poetry. Through reason, science; through irreason, religion. Through reason the market, the money, the rupees, the dollars; through irreason love, singing, dancing. No, it is good that man is not a rational being. Man is irrational.

Many definitions have been tried. I would like to say man is a gossip-creating animal. He creates myths—all myths are gossips, *puranas.* He creates religions, myths, stories about existence. Since the very beginning of humanity man has been creating beautiful mythology. He creates God. He creates that God created the world; and he creates beautiful myths. He weaves, goes on weaving newer and newer myths around and around. Man is a myth-creating animal; and life will be absolutely boring if there is no myth around it.

That is the trouble for the modern age: all the old myths have been dropped. Foolish rationalists argued too much against them. They have been dropped because if you argue against a myth, the myth is indefensible. It cannot defend itself. It is very vulnerable; it is very delicate. If you start fighting with it you will destroy it, but by destroying it you will destroy something beautiful in the human heart. It is not the myth, myth is just symbolic—deep are the roots in the heart. If you kill the myth you kill the heart.

Now, all over the world, those same rationalists who killed all the myths feel that now there is no meaning in life, no poetry, no reason to be happy, no cause to celebrate. All festivity has disappeared. Without a myth the world will be just a marketplace; all temples will disappear. Without myth all relationships will be bargains; there will be no love in them. Without myth you will be alone in vast emptiness.

Unless you are enlightened you cannot live that way; otherwise you will feel meaningless, and deep anxiety will arise and anguish will enter into your being. You will start committing suicide. You will start finding some way or other—drugs, alcohol, sex, anything—to drown yourself so you can forget yourself because life seems to be meaningless.

Myth gives meaning. Myth is nothing but a beautiful gossip, but it helps you to live. Unless you become so capable of living without any gossiping, it helps you to travel, to journey in the world. It gives a human atmosphere around you; otherwise the world is very stony. Just think: Indians go to the rivers, to the Ganges—they worship. That is a myth; otherwise the Ganges is just a river. But through a myth the Ganges becomes the mother, and when a Hindu goes to the Ganges it is a tremendous delight to him.

The stone in Mecca, the stone of Kaaba, is nothing but a stone.

It is a cube, that's why it is called *ka'bah*: *ka'bah* means cube. But you cannot know how a Muslim feels when he goes to Kaaba. Tremendous energy arises. Not that Kaaba is doing something—there is nothing, just a myth. But when he kisses the stone, he is not walking on the earth; he has moved in another world, the world of poetry. When he walks around the Kaaba, he is walking around God himself. All over the world Muslims pray; their direction is toward Kaaba. The direction differs depending on where they are: somebody praying in England will be looking at Kaaba; somebody praying in India will be looking at Kaaba; somebody praying in Egypt will be looking at Kaaba. Five times a day the Mohammedans pray all over the world, encircle the whole world, and they look at the Kaaba—the Kaaba becomes the very center of the world. A myth, a beautiful myth . . . in that moment the whole world is surrounded with poetry.

Human beings give meaning to existence; that's what a myth is all about. Man is a gossip-creating animal. Small gossips, just about the neighborhood, about the neighbor's wife . . . and big gossips, cosmic, about God. But people enjoy it.

I love one story; I must have told it many times. It is a Jewish story:

In a certain town, many centuries ago, one rabbi lived. Whenever there was some difficulty in the town, he would go to the forest, do some sacrifice, pray, follow a ritual, and tell God, "Avert that calamity. Save us." And the town was always saved.

This rabbi died; another man became the rabbi. The town was in difficulty; the people gathered. The rabbi went to the forest, but he could not find the place. He did not know it. So he said to God, "I don't know the exact place where the old rabbi used to pray to you, but that doesn't matter. You know the place, so I will pray from here." The trouble never came to the town. People were happy.

Then this rabbi died; another rabbi followed. Again the town was in some trouble, some calamity. People gathered. He went to the forest, but he said to God, "I don't know exactly where the place is, I don't know the ritual. I only know the prayer. So please, you are all-knowing, so don't be a stickler about the details. Listen to me . . ." And he said whatsoever he wanted to say. The calamity was avoided.

Then he also died; another rabbi followed. The town gathered, there was some trouble, some disease was spreading, and they said, "Go to the forest; it has always been done. Ancient rabbis have always been going there."

He was sitting in his armchair. He said, "What is the need to go there? He can hear from here. And I don't know where the place is . . ." So he looked at the skies and said, "Listen. I don't know the place, I don't know the ritual—I don't even know the prayer. I know the whole story of how the first rabbi used to go, how the second rabbi used to go, how the third, how the fourth . . . I will tell you the story—and I know you love stories. Please, listen to the story and avoid the trouble."

And he told the whole story about the ancient rabbis. And it is said God loved the story so much that the town was saved.

God must love stories so much; he is a creator of myths himself, he must love stories. He is the first one who started the whole gossip!

Yes, life is a gossip, a momentary gossip in the eternal silence of existence, and man is a gossip-creating animal. Unless you become a god you will have to love gossiping: you will love stories of Rama and Sita, of Adam and Eve, of the *Mahabharata*; you will love Greek, Roman, Chinese stories. Millions of them exist—all beautiful.

If you don't bring logic to them, they can reveal inner doors; they can open inner mysteries. If you bring logic to them, doors are closed; then that temple is not for you. Love stories. When you love them they open their mysteries. And much is hidden in them: all that humanity has found has been hidden in the parables. That's why Jesus goes on talking in parables, Buddha goes on talking in stories. They all loved gossiping.

The Man Who Loved Seagulls

Walking the Tightrope

A story of two criminals and their king

On belief
and trust,
and the
differences
between
them

Once, when the hasidim were seated together
in all brotherliness,
pipe in hand, Rabbi Israel joined them.
Because he was so friendly they asked him,
"Tell us, dear Rabbi, how should we serve God?"

He was surprised at the question,
and replied, "How should I know?"
But then he went on to tell them this story:

There were two friends of the king,
and both were proved guilty of a crime.
Since he loved them the king wanted to show them mercy,

but he could not acquit them because even a king's word
cannot prevail over the law.
So he gave this verdict:
A rope was to be stretched over a deep chasm,
and, one after another, the two were to walk across it.
Whoever reached to the other side was to be granted his life.
It was done as the king ordered,
and the first of the friends got safely across.

The other, still standing on the same spot, cried to him,
"Tell me, friend, how did you manage to cross?"

The first called back,
"I don't know anything but this:
Whenever I felt myself toppling over to one side,
I leaned to the other."[1]

Existence is paradoxical; paradox is its very core. It exists
through opposites, it is a balance in the opposites. And one who
learns how to balance becomes capable of knowing what life is,
what existence is, what God is. The secret key is balance.

A few things before we enter into this story . . . First, we have
been trained in Aristotelian logic—which is linear, one-
dimensional. Life is not Aristotelian at all, it is Hegelian. Logic is
not linear, logic is dialectical. The very process of life is dialectic,
a meeting of the opposites—a conflict between the opposites and
yet a meeting of the opposites. And life goes through this dialectical process: from thesis to antithesis, from antithesis to

[1] From *Tales of the Hasidim: The Early Masters/The Later Masters* by Martin Buber, translated by Olga Marx, copyright © 1947, 1948, copyright renewed 1975 by Schocken
Books. Used by permission of Schocken Books, a division of Random House, Inc.

synthesis—and then again the synthesis becomes a thesis. The whole process starts again.

If Aristotle is true then there will be only men and no women, or, only women and no men. If the world was made according to Aristotle then there will be only light and no darkness, or, only darkness and no light. That would be logical. There would be either life or death but not both.

But life is not based on Aristotle's logic, life has both. And life is really possible only because of both, because of the opposites: man and woman, yin and yang, day and night, birth and death, love and hate. Life consists of both.

This is the first thing you have to allow to sink deep into your heart—because Aristotle is in everybody's head. The whole education system of the world believes in Aristotle—although for the very advanced scientific minds Aristotle is out of date. He no longer applies. Science has gone beyond Aristotle because science has come closer to existence. And now science understands that life is dialectical, not logical.

I have heard.

Do you know that on Noah's ark, making love was forbidden while on board?

When the couples filed out of the ark after the flood, Noah watched them leave. Finally the tomcat and the she-cat left, followed by a number of very young kittens. Noah raised his eyebrows questioningly and the tomcat said to him, "You thought we were fighting!"

Noah must have been Aristotelian; the tomcat knew better.

Love is a sort of fight, love IS a fight. Without fight love cannot exist. They look opposite—because we think lovers should never fight. It is logical: if you love somebody how can you fight? It is absolutely clear, obvious to the intellect, that lovers should never fight—but they do. In fact, they are intimate enemies; they are continuously fighting. In that very fight the energy that is called love is released. Love is not only fight, love is not only struggle, that's true—it is more than that. It is fight too, but love transcends. The fight cannot destroy it. Love survives fight but it cannot exist without it.

Look into life: life is non-Aristotelian, non-Euclidean. If you don't force your concepts on life, if you simply look at things as they are, then you will be suddenly surprised to see that opposites are complementaries. And the tension between the opposites is the very basis on which life exists—otherwise it would disappear. Think of a world where death does not exist. . . . Your mind may say "then life will be there eternally," but you are wrong. If death does not exist life will simply disappear. It cannot exist without death; death gives it the background, death gives it color and richness, death gives it passion and intensity.

So death is not against life—the first thing—death is involved in life. And if you want to live authentically you have to learn how to continuously die authentically. You have to keep a balance between birth and death and you have to remain just in the middle. That remaining in the middle cannot be a static thing: it is not that once you have attained to a thing—finished, then there is nothing to be done. That is nonsense. One never achieves balance forever, one has to achieve it again and again and again.

This is very difficult to understand because our minds have been cultivated in concepts that are not applicable to real life. You think that once you have attained meditation then there is no need of anything more, then you will be in meditation. You are wrong. Meditation is not a static thing. It is a balance. You will have to attain it again and again and again. You will become more and more capable of attaining it, but it is not going to remain forever, like a possession in your hands. It has to be claimed each moment—only then is it yours. You cannot rest, you cannot say, "I have meditated and I have realized that now there is no need for me to do anything more. I can rest." Life does not believe in rest; it is a constant movement from perfection to more perfection.

Listen to me: from perfection to more perfection. It is never imperfect, it is always perfect, but always more perfection is possible. Logically these statements are absurd.

I was reading an anecdote. . . .

A man was charged with using counterfeit money to pay a bill. At his hearing, the defendant pleaded that he didn't know the money was phony. Pressed for proof, he admitted: "Because I stole it. Would I be stealing money that I knew was counterfeit?"

After thinking it over, the judge decided that made good sense, so he then tossed out the counterfeit charge. But he substituted a new charge—theft.

"Sure, I stole it," the defendant conceded amiably. "But counterfeit money has no legal value. Since when is it a crime to steal nothing?"

No one could find any flaw in his logic, so the man went free.

But logic won't do in life. You cannot go free so easily.

You can come out of a legal trap legally and logically because the trap consists of Aristotelian logic—you can use the same logic to come out of it. But in life you will not be able to come out because of logic, because of theology, because of philosophy, because you are very clever—clever in inventing theories. You can come out of life or you can go beyond life only through actual experience.

There are two types of people who are religious. The first type is childish; it is searching for a father figure. The first type is immature; it cannot rely upon itself, hence it needs a God somewhere or other. The God may exist or not—that is not the point—but a God is needed. Even if the God is not there the immature mind will invent him, because the immature mind has a psychological need—it is not a question of truth whether God is there or not, it is a psychological need.

In the Bible it is said God made man in his own image, but the reverse is more true: man made God in his own image. Whatsoever is your need you create that sort of God, that's why the concept of God goes on changing in every age. Every country has its own concept because every country has its own need. In fact, every single person has a different concept of God because his own needs are there and they have to be fulfilled.

So the first type of religious person—the so-called religious person—is simply immature. His religion is not religion but psychology. And when religion is psychology it is just a dream, a wish fulfillment, a desire. It has nothing to do with reality.

I was reading. . . .

A small boy was saying his prayers and concluded with this remark, "Dear God, take care of Mommy, take care of Daddy, take care of baby sister and Aunt Emma and Uncle John and Grandma and Grandpa—and, please God, take care of yourself, or else we're all sunk!"

This is the God of the majority. Ninety percent of the so-called religious people are immature people. They believe because they cannot live without belief; they believe because belief gives a sort of security; they believe because belief helps them to feel protected. It is *their* dream, but it helps. In the dark night of life, in the deep struggle of existence, without such a belief they will feel left alone. But their God is *their* God, not the godliness of reality. And once they get rid of their immaturity, their God will disappear.

That's what has happened to many people. In this century many people have become irreligious—not that they have come to know that God does not exist but only because this age has made man a little more mature. Man has come of age; man has become a little more mature. So the God of the childhood, the God of the immature mind, has simply become irrelevant.

That is the meaning when Friedrich Nietzsche declares that "God is dead." It is not godliness that is dead, it is the God of the immature mind that is dead. In fact, to say that God is dead is not right because that God was never alive. The only right expression will be to say that God is no longer relevant. Man can rely more upon himself—he does not need belief, he does not need the crutches of belief.

Hence people have become less and less interested in religion. They have become indifferent to what goes on in the church. They have become so indifferent to it that they will not even argue against it. If you say, "Do you believe in God?" they will say, "It's okay—whether he exists or not, it doesn't make any difference, it doesn't matter." Just to be polite, if you believe, they will say, "Yes, he exists." If you don't believe, they will say, "No, he does not exist." But it is no longer a passionate concern.

This is the first type of religion; it has existed for centuries, down the centuries, down the ages, and it is becoming more and more outmoded, out of date. Its time is finished. A new God is needed, which is not psychological; a new God is needed that is existential, the godliness of reality, the God *as* reality. We can even drop the word "God"—"the real" will do, "the existential" will do.

Then there is a second type of religious people for whom religion is not coming out of fear. The first type of religion comes out of fear, the second type—also bogus, also pseudo, also so-called—is not out of fear, it is only out of cleverness. There are very clever people who go on inventing theories, who are very trained in logic, in metaphysics, in philosophy. They create a religion that is just an abstraction: a beautiful piece of artwork, of intelligence, of intellectuality, of philosophizing. But it never penetrates life, it never touches life anywhere, it simply remains an abstract conceptualization.

Once Mulla Nasruddin was saying to me, "I have never been what I oughta been. I stole chickens and watermelons, got drunk and got in fights with my fists and my razor, but there is one thing I ain't never done: in spite of all my meanness I ain't never lost my religion."

Now what kind of religion is that? It has no impact on your life. You believe, but that belief never penetrates your life, never transforms it. It never becomes an intrinsic part of you, it never circulates in your blood, you never breathe it in or breathe it out, it never beats in your heart—it is simply something useless. Ornamental maybe, at the most, but of no utility to you. Some days you go to the church; it is a formality, a social need. And you can pay lip service to God, to the Bible, to the Koran, to the Vedas, but you don't mean it, you are not sincere about it. Your life goes on without it, your life goes on in a totally different way—it has nothing to do with religiousness.

Watch . . . somebody says he is a Mohammedan, somebody says he is a Hindu, somebody says he is a Christian, somebody says he is a Jew—their beliefs are different, but watch their lives and you will not find any difference. The Mohammedan, the Jew, the Christian, the Hindu—they all live the same life. Their life is not at all touched by their belief.

In fact, beliefs cannot touch your life, beliefs are devices. Beliefs are cunning devices through which you say "I know what life is"—and you can rest at ease, you are not troubled by life. You hold a concept and that concept helps you to rationalize. Then life does not bother you much because you have all the answers to all the questions.

But remember . . . unless religion is personal, unless religion is not abstract but real, deep in your roots, deep in your guts— unless it is like blood and bone and marrow—it is futile, it is of no use. It is the religion of philosophers not the religion of sages.

When the third type comes in . . . and that is the real type, these other two are the falsifications of religion, pseudo dimensions. Cheap, very easy, because they don't challenge you. The third is very difficult, arduous; it is a great challenge; it will create a turmoil in your life—because the third, the real religion says God has to be addressed in a personal way. You have to provoke him and you have to allow him to provoke you and you have to come to terms with him; in fact, you have to struggle with him, you have to clash against him. You have to love him, and you have to hate him; you have to be a friend and you have to be an enemy; you have to make your experience of God a living experience.

I have heard about a small child—and I would like you to be like this small child. He was really smart. . . .

A little boy was lost at a Sunday school picnic. His mother began a frantic search for him, and soon she heard loud sounds in a childish voice calling, "Estelle, Estelle!"

She quickly spotted the youngster and rushed up to grab him in her arms. "Why did you keep calling me by my name, Estelle, instead of Mother?" she asked him, as he had never called her by her first name before.

"Well," the youngster answered, "it was no use calling out 'Mother'—the place is full of them."

If you call "mother" there are so many mothers—the place is full of them. You have to call in a personal way, you have to call the first name.

Unless God is also called in a personal way, addressed with a first name, it will never become a reality in your life. You can go on calling "father" but whose father are you talking about? When Jesus called him "father" it was a personal address. When you use that word, it is absolutely impersonal. It is Christian but impersonal. When Jesus called him "father" it was meaningful; when you talk about the "father" it is meaningless—you have made no contact, no real contact with existence. Only an experience of life—neither belief nor philosophy—only an experience of life will make you able to address existence in a personal way. Then you can encounter it.

And unless existence is encountered you are simply deceiving yourself with words . . . with words which are empty, hollow, with words which have no content.

There was a very famous Sufi mystic, Shaqiq was his name. He trusted God so deeply, so tremendously, that he lived only out of that trust. Jesus says to his disciples, "Look at those lilies in the field—they labor not and yet they are so beautiful and so alive that not even Solomon was so beautiful in all his glory." Shaqiq lived the life of a lily. There have been very few mystics who have lived that way, but there have been ordinary people who have lived that way. The trust is so infinite, the trust is so absolute that there is no need to do anything—existence goes on doing things for you: in fact, even when you are doing them God is doing them; it is only that you think you are doing them.

One day a man came to Shaqiq accusing him of idleness, laziness, and asked him to work for him. "I will pay you according to your services," the man added.

Shaqiq replied, "I would accept your offer if it weren't for five drawbacks. First, you might go broke. Second, thieves might steal your wealth. Third, whatever you give me you will do so grudgingly. Fourth, if you find faults with my work, you'll probably fire me. Fifth, should death come to you, I'll lose the source of my sustenance.

"Now," Shaqiq concluded, "it happens that I have a Master who is totally devoid of such imperfections."

This is what trust is. Trust in life then you cannot lose anything. But that trust cannot come by indoctrination, that trust cannot come by education, preaching, studying, thinking—that trust can only come by experiencing life in all its opposites, in all its contradictions, in all its paradoxes. When within all the paradoxes you come to the point of balance, there is trust. Trust is a perfume of balance, the fragrance of balance.

If you really want to attain to trust, drop all your beliefs. They will not help. A believing mind is a stupid mind; a trusting mind has pure intelligence in it. A believing mind is a mediocre mind; a trusting mind becomes perfect. Trust makes perfect.

And the difference between belief and trust is simple. I am not talking about the dictionary meaning of the words—in the dictionary it may be so: belief means trust, trust means faith, faith means belief—I am talking about existence. In an existential way belief is borrowed, trust is yours. Belief you believe in but doubt exists just underneath. Trust has no doubt element in it; it is simply devoid of doubt. Belief creates a division in you: a part of your mind believes, a part of your mind denies. Trust is a unity in your being, your totality.

But how can your totality trust unless you have experienced it? The God of Jesus won't do, the God of my experience won't do for you, the God of Buddha's experience won't do—it has to be *your* experience. And if you carry beliefs you will come again and again to experiences which don't fit the belief, and then there is the tendency of the mind not to see those experiences, not to take note of them because they are very disturbing. They destroy your belief and you want to cling to your belief. Then you become more and more blind to life—belief becomes a blindfold on the eyes.

Trust opens the eyes; trust has nothing to lose. Trust means whatsoever is real is real—"I can put my desires and wishes aside, they don't make any difference to reality. They can only distract my mind from reality."

If you have a belief and you come against an experience that the belief says is not possible, or, the experience is such that you have to drop the belief, what are you going to choose—the belief or the experience? The tendency of the mind is to choose the belief, to forget about the experience. That's how you have been missing many opportunities when God has knocked at your door.

Remember, it is not only you who are seeking truth—truth is also seeking you. Many times the hand has come very close to you, it has almost touched you, but you shrugged yourself away. It was not fitting with your belief and you chose to choose your belief.

I have heard a very beautiful Jewish joke.

There is a joke about a vampire who flew into Patrick O'Rourke's bedroom one night for the purpose of drinking his blood. Remembering the stories his mother told him, O'Rourke

grabbed a crucifix and brandished it frantically in the vampire's
face. The vampire paused for a moment, shook his head consol-
ingly, clucked his tongue, and commented genially in the purest
Yiddish, "Oy vey, bubbula! Have you ever got the wrong vampire!"
    Now, if the vampire is Christian, good! You can show the
cross. But if the vampire is Jewish. then what? Then "Oy vey,
bubbula! Have you ever got the wrong vampire!"

If you have a certain belief and life does not fit with it, what are you
going to do? You can go on showing your crucifix—but if the vampire is a Jew, he is not going to take any note of your cross. Then
what are you going to do?

Life is so vast and beliefs are so small; life is so infinite and beliefs are so tiny. Life never fits with any belief, and if you try to
force life into your beliefs you are trying to do the impossible. It
has never happened; it cannot happen in the nature of things.
Drop all beliefs and start learning how to experience.

Now this story.

Once when the hasidim were seated together
in all brotherliness,
pipe in hand, Rabbi Israel joined them.
Because he was so friendly they asked him,
"Tell us, dear Rabbi, how should we serve God?"

A few things about Hasidism. First, the word *"hasid"* comes
from a Hebrew word which means pious, pure. It is derived from
the noun *"hased"* which means grace.

This word "hasid" is very beautiful. The whole standpoint of Hasidism is based on grace. It is not that *you* do something—life is already happening, you just be silent, passive, alert, receiving. God comes through his grace, not through your effort. So Hasidism has no austerities prescribed for you. Hasidism believes in life, in joy. Hasidism is one of the religions in the world which is life affirmative. It has no renunciation in it; you are not to renounce anything. Rather, you have to celebrate. The founder of Hasidism, Baal-Shem, is reported to have said, "I have come to teach you a new way. It is not fasting and penance, and it is not indulgence, but joy in God."

The Hasid loves life, tries to experience life. That very experience starts giving you a balance. And in that state of balance, someday, when you are really balanced, neither leaning on this side nor leaning on that side, when you are exactly in the middle, you transcend. The middle is the beyond, the middle is the door from where one goes beyond.

If you really want to know what existence is, it is neither in life nor in death. Life is one extreme, death is another extreme. It is just exactly in the middle where neither death is nor life is, where one is simply unborn, deathless. In that moment of balance, equilibrium, grace descends.

I would like you all to become receivers of grace. I would like you to learn this science, this art of balance.

The mind very easily chooses the extreme. There are people who indulge: they indulge in sensuality, sexuality, food, clothes, houses, this and that. There are people who indulge—they lean too much toward life, they fall down, they topple. Then there are people who, seeing people toppling down from the tightrope of existence into indulgence, falling into the abyss of indulgence, become afraid; they start leaning toward the other extreme. They renounce the world, they escape to the Himalayas. They escape from the wife, the children, the home, the world, the marketplace, and they go and hide themselves in monasteries. They have chosen another extreme. Indulgence is the extreme life; renunciation is the extreme death.

So there is some truth in Friedrich Nietzsche's comment upon Hinduism—that Hinduism is a religion of death. There is some truth when Nietzsche says that Buddha seems to be suicidal. The truth is this: you can move from one extreme to another.

The whole Hasidic approach is not to choose any extreme, just to remain in the middle, available to both and yet beyond both, not getting identified with either, not getting obsessed and fixated with either—just remaining free and joyously enjoying both. If life comes, enjoy life; if death comes, enjoy death. If out of his grace God gives love, life—good; if he sends death, it must be good—it is his gift.

Baal-Shem is right when he says, "I have come to teach you joy in God." Hasidism is a celebrating religion. It is the purest flowering of the whole Judaic culture. Hasidism is the fragrance of the whole Jewish race. It is one of the most beautiful phenomena on the earth.

Once when the hasidim were sitting together in all brotherliness . . .

Hasidism teaches life in community. It is a very communal approach. It says that man is not an island, man is not an ego—should not be an ego, should not be an island. Man should live a life of community.

We are growing a Hasidic community here. To live in a community is to live in love; to live in a community is to live in commitment, caring for others.

There are many religions which are very, very self-oriented: they only think of the self, they never think of the community. They only think of how I am going to become liberated, how I am going to become free, how I should attain moksha—*my moksha, my* freedom, *my* liberation, *my* salvation. But everything is preceded by "*my*," by the self. And these religions try hard to drop the ego but their whole effort is based on the ego. Hasidism says if you want to drop the ego, the best way is to live in a community, live with people, be concerned with people—with their joy, with their sadness, with their happiness, with their life, with their death. Create a concern for the others, be involved, and then the ego will disappear on its own accord. And when the ego is not, one is free. There is no freedom of the ego, there is only freedom *from* the ego.

Hasidism uses community life as a device. Hasids have lived in small communities and they have created beautiful communities, very celebrating, dancing, enjoying the small things of life. They make the small things of life holy—eating, drinking. Everything takes the quality of prayer. The ordinariness of life is no longer ordinary, it is suffused with divine grace.

Once when the hasidim were sitting together in all
brotherliness . . .

This is the difference. If you see Jaina monks sitting, you never see any brotherliness—it is not possible. The very approach is different. Each Jaina monk is an island, but the Hasids are not islands. They are a continent, a deep brotherliness.

A man alone, confined to himself, is ugly. Life is in love, life is in flow, in give and take and sharing.

You can go to a Jaina monastery or a Jaina temple where Jaina monks are sitting—you can just watch. You will see exactly how everybody is confined to himself; there is no relationship. That is the whole effort: how not to be related. The whole effort is how to disconnect all relationship. But the more you are disconnected from community and life, the more dead you are. It is very difficult to find a Jaina monk who is still alive. And I know it very deeply because I was born a Jaina and I have watched them from my very childhood. I was simply surprised! What calamity has happened to these people? What has gone wrong? They are dead. They are corpses. If you don't go near them already prejudiced, thinking that they are great saints—if you simply go, observing without any prejudice—you will be simply puzzled, confused. What illness, what disease has happened to these people? They are neurotic. Their concern about themselves has become their neurosis.

Community has completely lost meaning for them—but all meaning is in community. Remember . . . when you love somebody, it is not only that you give love to them—in giving, you grow. When love starts flowing between you and the other, you both are benefited. And in that exchange of love your potentialities start becoming actualities. That's how self-actualization happens. Love more and you will be more; love less and you will be less. You are always in proportion to your love. The proportion of your love is the proportion of your being.

Once when the hasidim were seated together in all
brotherliness,
    pipe in hand . . .

Can you think of any saint with a pipe in hand?

. . . pipe in hand, Rabbi Israel joined them.

Ordinary life has to be hallowed, has to be made holy, even a pipe. You can smoke in a very prayerful way. Or you can pray in a very unprayerful way. It is not a question of what you do . . . you can go into the temple, you can go into the mosque, but still you can pray in a very unprayerful way. It depends on you; it depends on the quality you bring to your prayer. You can eat, you can smoke, you can drink, and you can do all these small things, mundane things, in such gratitude that they become prayers.

The point is this: it does not depend on what you do. You can touch somebody's feet in a very unprayerful way; then it is meaningless; but you can smoke and you can do it in a prayerful way and your prayer will reach to God.

It is very difficult for people who have very fixed concepts about religion, spirituality, but I would like you to become more liquid. Don't have fixed concepts. Watch.

. . . pipe in hand, Rabbi Israel joined them.

Because he was so friendly they asked him, "Tell us, dear Rabbi, how should we serve God?"

Yes, only in deep friendliness can something be asked. And only in deep friendliness can something be answered. Between the Master and the disciple there is a deep friendship. It is a love affair. And the disciple has to wait for the right moment and the Master has also to wait for the right moment; when the friendship is flowing, when there is no hindrance, then things can be answered. Or even, sometimes, without answering them, they can be answered; even without using verbalization the message can be delivered.

He was surprised at the question, and replied, "How should I know?"

In fact, that is the answer of all those who know. "How should I know?"

"How to serve God? You are asking such a great question, I am not worthy to answer it," said the Master. "How should I know?"

Nothing can be known about love; nothing can be known about how to serve God—it is very difficult.

But then he went on to tell them this story . . .

First he says, "How should I know?" First he says that knowledge is not possible about such things. First he says that he cannot give you any knowledge about such things. First he says that he cannot make you more knowledgeable about these things—there is no way. But then he tells his story.

A story is totally different from talking in terms of theories. A story is more alive, more indicative. It does not say much but it shows much. And all the great Masters have used stories, parables, anecdotes. The reason is that if you say something directly, it kills much. A direct expression is too crude, primitive, gross, ugly. The parable is saying the thing in a very indirect way. It makes things very smooth; it makes things more poetic, less logical, closer to life, more paradoxical. You cannot use a syllogism for God, you cannot use any argument, but you can tell stories.

And the Jewish race is one of the richest races on the earth for parables. Jesus was a Jew and he has told a few of the most beautiful parables ever uttered. Jews have learned how to tell stories. In fact, Jews don't have much philosophy but they have beautiful philosophical parables. They say much; without saying, without hinting anything directly, they create an atmosphere. In that atmosphere something can be understood. That is the whole device of a parable.

But then he went on to tell them this story . . .

First he says, "How should I know?" First he simply denies knowledge of any possibility of knowing about it. A philosopher says, "Yes, I know" and a philosopher proposes a theory in clear-cut statements, logical, mathematical, syllogistic, argumentative. He tries to convince. He may not convince but he can force you into silence.

A parable never tries to convince you. It takes you unawares, it persuades you, it tickles you deep inside.

The moment the Master says, "How should I know?" he is saying to them, "Relax, I am not going to give any argument for it, any theory for it. And you need not be worried that I am going to convince you about something. Just enjoy a little parable, a little story." When you start listening to a story, you relax; when you start listening to a theory, you become tense. And that which creates tension in you cannot be of much help. It is destructive.

But then he went on to tell them this story. . . .
There were two friends of the king,

and both were proved guilty of a crime.
Since he loved them the king wanted to show them mercy,
but he could not acquit them because even a king's word
cannot prevail over the law.
So he gave this verdict:
A rope was to be stretched over a deep chasm,
and, one after another, the two were to walk across it.
Whoever reached to the other side was to be granted his life.

A parable has an atmosphere, a very homely atmosphere—as
if your grandmother is telling you a story when you are falling
asleep. Children ask, "Tell us stories." It helps them relax and go
into sleep. A story is very relaxing and does not create any pres-
sure on your mind; rather, it starts playing with your heart. When
you listen to a story, you don't listen from the head—you cannot
listen to a story from the head—if you listen from the head you will
miss. If you listen from the head there is no possibility of understanding a story; a story has to be understood from the heart.
That's why races and countries which are very "heady" cannot understand beautiful jokes. For example, Germans! They cannot understand. They are one of the most intelligent races of the world
but they don't have any good stock of jokes.

> *A man was telling a German—I have just overheard this—a man
> was telling a German that he had heard a very beautiful Ger-
> man joke.*
>
> *The German said, "But remember, I am a German."*
>
> *So the man said, "Okay, then I will tell it very, very slowly."*

It is very difficult. Germany is the country of the professors,
logicians—Kant, Hegel, and Feuerbach—and they have always
been thinking through the head. They have cultivated the head,

they have created great scientists, logicians, philosophers, but they have missed something.

In India we don't have many jokes; there is a great poverty of spirit. You cannot find a specifically Hindu joke, no. All the jokes that are told in India are borrowed from the West. No Indian joke exists. I have not come across any. And you can rely on me because I have come across all the jokes of the world! No Hindu joke, as such, exists. What is the reason? Again, very intellectual people. They have been weaving and spinning theories; from Vedas to Sarvapalli Radhakrishnan they have been just weaving and spinning theories and theories and they have got into it so deeply that they have forgotten how to tell a beautiful story or how to create a joke.

The Rabbi started telling this story—the disciples must have become relaxed, must have become relaxed *and* attentive. That's the beauty of a story: when a story is told you are attentive and yet not tense. You can relax and yet you are attentive. A passive attentiveness arises when you listen to a story. When you listen to a theory you become very tense because if you miss a single word you may not be able to understand it. You become more concentrated. When you listen to a story you become more meditative—there is nothing much to be lost. Even if a few words are lost here and there, nothing will be lost because if you just have the feel of the story you will understand it, it does not depend so much on the words.

The disciples must have relaxed, and the Master told this story.

So he gave this verdict:
A rope was to be stretched over a deep chasm,
and, one after another, the two were to walk across it.
Whoever reached to the other side was to be granted his life.

Now, this sentence is very pregnant—

Whoever reached to the other side was to be granted his life.

Jesus says many times to his disciples, "Come unto me if you want life in abundance. If you want life in abundance, come to me." But life in abundance happens only to people who go beyond birth and death, who go beyond the duality, to the other shore. The other shore, the other side, is just symbolic of the transcendental. But it is just a hint. Nothing is particularly said, just a hint is given. And then the story moves on.

It was done as the king ordered, and the first of the friends got safely across.

Now these are the two types of people.

The first simply got safely across. Ordinarily we would like to inquire how to go on a rope. A tightrope stretched over a chasm—it is dangerous. Ordinarily we would like to know the ways, the means, the method, how to go. We would like to know how? The technique—there must be a technique. For centuries people have walked on tightropes.

But the first one simply walked without inquiring, without even waiting for the other. This is the natural tendency: to let the other go first. At least you will be able to watch and observe and that will be helpful for you. No, the first simply walked. He must have been a man of tremendous trust; he must have been a man of undoubting confidence. He must have been a man who has learned one thing in life: that there is only one way to learn and that is to live, to experience. There is no other way.

You cannot learn tightrope walking by watching a tightrope walker—no, never. Because the thing is not like a technology that you can observe from the outside, it is some inner balance that only the walker knows. And it cannot be transferred. He cannot just tell you about it; it cannot be verbalized. No tightrope walker can tell anybody how he manages.

You ride a bicycle. Can you tell anybody how you ride it? You know the balance; it is a sort of tightrope-walking, just on two wheels straight in one line. And you go fast and you go so trustingly. If somebody asks what the secret is, can you reduce it to a formula, just like H_2O? Can you reduce it to a maxim? You don't say, "This is the principle, I follow this principle," you will say, "The only way is for you to come and sit on the bike and I will help you to go on it. You are bound to fall a few times and then you will know the only way to know is to know." The only way to know swimming is to swim—with all the dangers involved in it.

The first man must have come to a deep understanding in his life—that life is not like a textbook. You cannot be taught about it, you have to experience it. And he must have been a man of tremendous awareness. He did not hesitate, he simply walked, as if he had always been walking on a tightrope. He had never walked before; it was for the first time.

But for a man of awareness everything is for the first time, and a man of awareness can do things—even when he is doing them for the first time—perfectly. His efficiency does not come out of his past, his efficiency comes out of his present. Let this be remembered. You can do things in two ways. You can do something because you have done it before—so you know how to do it, you need not be present, you can simply do it in a mechanical way. But if you have not done it before, and you are going to do it for a first time, you have to be tremendously alert because now you don't have any past experience. So you cannot rely on the memory, you have to rely on awareness.

These are the two sources of functioning: either you function out of memory, out of knowledge, out of the past, out of mind; or you function out of awareness, out of the present, out of no-mind.

The first man must have been a man of no-mind, a man who knows that you can simply be alert and go on and see what happens. And whatsoever happens is good. A great courage . . .

. . . The first of the friends got safely across. The other, still standing on the same spot, cried to him, "Tell me, friend, how did you manage to cross?"

The second is the majority mind, the mass mind. The second wants to know first how to cross it. Is there a method to it? Is there a technique to be learned? He is waiting for the other to say.

"Tell me, friend, how did you manage to cross?"

The other must be a believer in knowledge. The other must have been a believer in others' experiences.

Many people come to me. They say, "Osho, tell us. What happened to you?" But what are you going to do about it? Buddha has told it, Mahavir has told it, Jesus has told it—what have you done about it? Unless it happens to you it is futile. I can tell you one more story and then you can join that story also in your record of memories, but that is not going to help.

Waiting for others' knowledge is waiting in vain because that which can be given by the others has no worth, and that which is of any worth cannot be given and cannot be transferred.

The first called back, "I don't know anything but this. . . ."

Even though he had crossed he still said, "I don't know anything but this. . . ." Because, in fact, life never becomes knowledge; it remains a very suffused experience, never knowledge. You cannot verbalize it, conceptualize it, put it into a clear-cut theory.

"I don't know anything but this: Whenever I felt myself toppling over to one side, I leaned to the other."

"This much only can be said: that there were two extremes, left and right, and whenever I felt that I was going too much toward the left and the balance was getting lost, I leaned toward the right. But again I had to balance because then I started going too much to the right and again I felt the balance was getting lost. Again I leaned toward the left."

So he said two things. One, "I cannot formulate it as knowledge. I can only indicate. I don't know exactly what happened but this much I can give as a hint to you. And that is not much; in fact, you need not have it. You will come across the experience yourself. But this much can be said."

Buddha was asked again and again, "What has happened to you?" And he would always say, "That cannot be said but this much I can say to you—I can say in what circumstances it happened. That may be of some help to you. I cannot tell about the ultimate truth but I can tell how, on what path, with what method, in what situation I was when it happened, when the grace descended on me, when the benediction came to me."

The man says,

_____

. . . Whenever I felt myself toppling over to one side, I leaned to the other."

_____

"That's all. Nothing much to it. That's how I balanced, that's how I remained in the middle." And in the middle is grace.

The Rabbi is saying to his disciples, "You ask how we should serve God?" He was indicating with this parable: remain in the middle.

Don't indulge too much and don't renounce too much. Don't be only in the world and don't escape out of it. Go on keeping a balance. When you feel that now you are falling into too much indulgence, lean toward renunciation, and when you feel that now you are going to become a renunciate, an ascetic, lean back again to indulgence. Keep in the middle.

On the road in India you will find signs saying "Keep to the Left"—in America you will find "Keep to the Right." In the world there are only two types of people: a few keep to the left, a few keep to the right. The third type is the very pinnacle of consciousness. And there, the rule is "Keep to the Middle." Don't try it on the road! But on life's way, keep to the middle. Never to the left, never to the right . . . just to the middle.

And in the middle there will be glimpses of balance. There is a point—you can understand, you can feel it—there is a point when you are not leaning to either extreme, you are exactly in the middle. In that split second suddenly there is grace, everything is in equilibrium.

And that's how one can serve God. Remain in balance and it becomes a service to God; remain in balance and God is available to you and you are available to God.

Life is not a technology, not even a science; life is an art—or it would even be better to call it a hunch. You have to feel it. It is like balancing on a tightrope.

The Rabbi has chosen a beautiful parable. He has not talked about God at all; he has not talked about service at all; he has not really answered the question at all directly. The disciples must have themselves forgotten about the question—that's the beauty of a parable. It doesn't divide your mind into a question and an answer, it simply gives you a hunch that this is how things are.

Life has no "know-how" about it. Remember, life is not American, it is not a technology. The American mind, or to be more specific, the modern mind, tends to create technologies out of everything. Even when there is meditation the modern mind immediately tends to create a technology out of it. Then we create machines, and man is getting lost, and we are losing all contact with life.

Remember, there are things which cannot be taught but which can only be caught. I am here, you can watch me, you can look into me and you will see a balance and you will see a silence. It is almost tangible, you can touch it, you can hear it, you can see it. It is here. I cannot say what it is, I cannot specifically give you techniques how to attain to it. At the most I can tell you a few parables, a few stories. They will be just hints. Those that understand will allow those hints to fall into their hearts like seeds. In their time, in the right season, they will sprout and you will understand me really only on the day you also experience the same that I am experiencing. I have crossed to the other shore, you are shouting from the other side, "Tell me, friend, how did you manage to cross?" I can tell you only one thing,

---

"I don't know anything but this: Whenever I felt myself toppling to the one side, I leaned to the other."

Keep to the middle. Keep continuously alert that you don't lose the balance, and then everything will take care of itself.

If you can remain in the middle, you remain available to God, to his grace. If you can remain in the middle you can become a Hasid; you can become a receiver of grace. And God is grace. You cannot do anything to find him, you can only do one thing: not stand in his way. And whenever you move to an extreme you become so tense that that very tension makes you too solid; whenever you are in the middle, tension disappears, you become liquid, fluid. And you are no longer in the way. When you are in the middle you are no longer in God's way—or let me tell you it in this way: when you are in the middle you are not. Exactly in the middle that miracle happens—that you are nobody, you are a nothingness.

This is the secret key. It can open the lock of mystery, of existence, to you.

Enough for today.

Mere Players of a Game

The angry samurai at the river crossing

On the self-inflicted miseries of ambition and impatience

Muso, the national teacher,
and one of the most illustrious masters of his day,
left the capital in the company of a disciple
for a distant province.

On reaching the Tenryu River
they had to wait for an hour
before they could board the ferry.
Just as the ferry was about to leave the shore
a drunken samurai ran up
and jumped into the packed boat,
nearly swamping it.

He tottered wildly as the small craft
made its way across the river.

The ferryman,
fearing for the safety of his passengers,
begged him to stand quietly.
"We're like sardines in here," said the samurai gruffly.
Then, pointing to Muso, "Why not toss out the bonzae?"
"Please be patient," Muso said,
"We'll reach the other side soon."
"What!" bawled the samurai. "Me be patient?
Listen here, if you don't jump off this thing
I swear I'll drown you."

The master's calm so infuriated the samurai
that he struck Muso's head with his iron fan,
drawing blood.

Muso's disciple had had enough by this time,
and as he was a powerful man,
wanted to challenge the samurai.
"I can't permit him to go on living after this," he said.
"Why get so worked up over a trifle?"
Muso said with a smile.
"It's exactly in matters of this kind
that the bonzae's training proves itself.
Patience, you must remember,
is more than just a word."

Then he recited an extempore waka:
"The beater and the beaten:
mere players of a game
ephemeral as a dream."

When the boat reached shore,
and Muso and his disciple alighted,
the samurai ran up
and prostrated himself at the master's feet.
Then and there he became a disciple.[2]

Seeking for something, desiring for something, is the basic disease of the mind. Not seeking, not desiring, is the basic health of your being.

It is very easy to go on changing the objects of desire, but that is not the way of transformation. You can desire money, you can desire power . . . you can change the objects of desire—you can start desiring God—but you remain the same because you go on desiring.

The basic change is to be brought not in the objects of desire, but in your subjectivity.

If desiring stops—and remember, I am not saying that it has to be stopped—if desiring stops, then you are for the first time at home, peaceful, patient, blissful, and for the first time life is available to you and you are available to life. In fact, the very division between you and life disappears, and this state of nondivision is the state of God.

People come to me from all over the world; they travel thousands of miles. When they come to me and I ask, "Why have you come?" somebody says, "I am a seeker of God." Somebody says, "I am a seeker of truth."

They are not aware what they are asking. They are asking the impossible. God is not a thing. God is not an object. You cannot

---

[2] From the book *Zen: Poems, Prayers, Sermons, Anecdotes, Interviews,* 2nd edition, selected and translated by Lucien Stryk and Takashi Ikemoto. Reprinted with the permission of Swallow Press/Ohio University Press, Athens, Ohio.

seek him. God is this whole. How can you seek the whole? You can dissolve in it, you can merge in it, but you cannot seek it. The seeking simply shows that you go on believing yourself separate from the whole—you the seeker and the whole the sought.

Sometimes you seek a woman, sometimes you seek a man. Sometimes, frustrated from the world, you start seeking the other world—but you are not yet frustrated with seeking itself.

A seeker is in trouble. A seeker is confused. He has not understood the basic problem itself. It is not that you have to seek god, then everything will be solved. Just the opposite—if everything is solved, suddenly there is god.

The seeking is a disease. Don't make it an ego trip . . . because when somebody comes and he says that he is a seeker after god, I can see the light of the ego that shows in his eyes; the condemnation of the world—that he is not a worldly man, he is a religious man. The way he says it shows his pride—that he is not an ordinary man, not part of the ordinary run of humanity. He is special, extraordinary. He is not seeking money, he is seeking meditation. He is not seeking anything material, he is seeking something spiritual.

But to me, and to all those who have ever known, seeking is the world. There is no otherworldly seeking. Desiring is worldly. There is no otherworldly desiring. In the very desiring, the world exists. What you desire is irrelevant; that you desire is enough to make you worldly. Because all desires are from a basic fallacy—the basic fallacy that you are missing something, that something is needed. In the very first place, you are not missing anything. Nothing is needed.

The world is a nightmare because of desiring, and then nirvana becomes the last nightmare. Of course the last, because if you wake up seeking god and nirvana . . . if you wake up, then all nightmares disappear.

You have dropped the world. Now you seek god. Please drop god also. This will look a little irreligious; it is not.

I was reading one statement of Albert Einstein. I loved it.

Somewhere he says, "I am a deeply religious unbeliever." In fact a religious person cannot be a believer. A religious person can trust, but cannot believe. Trust comes out of existential experience; belief is just a mind trip. Belief is just of ideology, concepts, scriptures, philosophy. Trust is of life.

The moment you say "god," you have used a belief. God is a belief. But life is not a belief, it is an experience. Let life be your only god. No other god is needed, because all other gods are human inventions. Einstein is true when he says, "I am a deeply religious person, but unbelieving, not a believer." What does he mean?

The quality of being religious has nothing to do with the quality of a believer. A believer believes because he desires. A believer believes because he wants to seek something. A believer believes because he cannot live life without the mind. He brings the mind always in between life and himself . . . as if your hand is hiding behind a glove—you touch your beloved, but not directly; your hand is hidden behind the glove. The glove touches the beloved; you touch your glove only.

A belief is like a glove; it surrounds you. You are never available to life directly, immediately.

A religious person is naked in this sense—he has no clothes of beliefs. He is simply direct, in touch with life.

In that touch, the melting. In that touch, the merging. In that touch, somewhere you are no more you. Somewhere you have become the whole and the whole has come to you. The ocean drops into the drop and the drop becomes the ocean.

Beliefs are dangerous. We go on changing beliefs. A Hindu can become a Mohammedan, a Christian can become a Hindu. Or a religious person, a so-called religious person, can become a communist; a theist can become an atheist—it makes no difference. You go on changing the glove, but the glove remains.

Can't you see life directly? Can't you love life directly? Is there really any need to believe in anything? Can't you trust life?

Let me say it in this way. People who cannot trust, believe.

Belief is a substitute; a false coin, a deception. People who can trust
need no beliefs. Life is enough. They don't overimpose any god,
any nirvana, any moksha on top of it. There is no need. Life is
more than enough. They live life.

Of course, if you have a belief, you can create a future around it.
If you don't have any belief then you don't have any future, because life is herenow. There is no need to wait. But we go on
postponing—to the very moment death comes and takes the gift
back.

I was reading:

"Three men were engaged in one of those profitless conversa-
tions which involve all of us at one time or another. They were
considering the problem of what each would do if the doctor told
him he had only six months to live.

"Said Robinson, 'If my doctor said I had only six months to
live, the first thing l would do would be to liquidate my business,
withdraw my savings, and have the biggest fling on the French
Riviera you ever saw. I would play roulette, I would eat like a king,
and most of all I would have girls, girls, and more girls.' "

This man must have been postponing—postponing for death.
When a doctor says you have only six months to live, then . . . But
that too seems to be just a wish, he may not be able—because when
death knocks at the door, one is so shocked and shattered. . . .
When death has come near you, how can you enjoy? You could not
enjoy when life was close. When life is receding farther away each
moment, how can you enjoy? This is again just a way of believing
that if it happens, then "immediately I will start living." Who is
preventing you from living right now?

"The second man said, 'If my doctor said I had only six months
to live, the first thing I would do would be to visit a travel agency
and plot out a world tour. There are thousands of places on earth I
have not seen and I would like to see them before I die—the Grand
Canyon, the Taj Mahal, Angkor Wat—all of them.' "

Who is preventing you? Why are you waiting for death to come and then you will go and see the Taj Mahal? Will you be able to see the Taj Mahal then? Your eyes will be so filled with darkness that the Taj Mahal won't look like a Taj Mahal. It will be impossible to see when death has come into the mind. It will make you blind. An inner trembling will overpower you. You will not be able to hear, you will not be able to see, you will not be able even to breathe. But why do people go on postponing?

"Said the third man, 'If my doctor said I had only six months to live, the first thing I would do would be to consult another doctor.'"

This seems to be the most representative of all men. This is what you are also going to do. You are not going to live even then. You will try another doctor who can again give you hope, who can again give you future, who can again tell you, "No need to be worried—you can still postpone. No need to be in a hurry—death is far away." You will find, you will seek someone, who can still give you hope.

Hope is a way of postponing life.

All desiring is a way of postponing life, and all beliefs are tricks how to avoid that which is and how to go on thinking about that which is not.

God is not. Life is. Please don't be seekers of god.

Nirvana is not. Life is. Please don't be seekers of nirvana.

And if you stop seeking nirvana, you will find nirvana hidden in life itself. If you stop seeking god, you will find god everywhere . . . in each particle, in each moment of life. God is another name of life. Nirvana is another name of life lived. You have just heard the word "life"; it is not a lived experience.

Drop all beliefs, they are hindrances. Don't be a Christian, don't be a Hindu, don't be a Mohammedan. Just be alive. Let that be your only religion.

Life—the only religion. Life—the only temple. Life—the only prayer.

I have heard, a disciple came to a Zen Master, bowed down,

touched his feet, and said, "How long do I have to wait for my enlightenment?"

The Master looked at him long, long enough. The disciple started getting restless. He repeated his question and he said, "Why are you looking at me so long? Why don't you answer me?"

And the Master answered a really Zen answer. He said, "Kill me."

The disciple could not believe that this was the answer for his enlightenment. He went to ask the chief disciple. The chief disciple laughed and he said, "The same he did to me also." And he is right. He is saying, "Why do you go on asking me? Drop this 'Master.' Drop this asking. Kill me. Drop all ideology. Who am I? I am not preventing you. Life is available. Why don't you start living? Why do you go on preparing, when and how?"

This seems to be the most difficult thing for the human mind—just to live, naked; just to live without any arrangements; just to live the raw and the wild life; just to live the moment.

And this is the whole teaching of all the great teachers, but you go on making philosophies out of them. Then you create a doctrine, and then you start believing in the doctrine.

There are many Zen people who believe in Zen—and Zen teaches trust, not belief. There are many people around me who believe in me—and I teach you trust, not belief. If you trust your life, you have trusted me. No intellectual belief is needed.

Let this truth go as deep in you as possible: that life is already here, arrived. You are standing on the goal. Don't ask about the path.

In Franz Kafka there is a parable; it looks like Zen, almost Zen. Kafka says,

> I was staying in a strange town. I was a new arrival there, and I had to catch a train early in the morning. But when I got up and looked at my watch, I was already late so I started running. When I came to the tower and looked at the tower-clock I became

even more afraid that I would miss my train, because my watch
was itself late. So I started running . . . not knowing the path,
not knowing the way . . . and the streets were clean and de-
serted. It was early in the morning, a cold winter morning, and I
couldn't see anybody.

Then suddenly I saw a policeman. Hope came into me. I
went to the policeman and I asked about the way, and the po-
liceman said, "The way? Why are you asking me?"

And I said to him, "I am a stranger in this town and I don't
know the way, that's why. Please show me the way, and don't
waste time—I am already late and I will miss the train, and it is
important to catch the train."

The policeman laughed and he said, "Who can show the
way to anybody else?"

The policeman said this, and he waved a hand and moved
away smiling.

Here ends the parable. It looks exactly Zen. In the West they
think this is surrealistic, absurd. It is not. Of course from a policeman it looks more absurd than from a Zen Master, but sometimes policemen can be Zen Masters.

Who can show you the way? Because basically the way does not
exist.

You are always on the goal. Wherever you are is the goal. The
way does not exist.

If you go on asking about the way, you are trying to create future again and again—and future is the nightmare.

Look. This very moment life is pouring from everywhere. A single moment of witnessing—and you will laugh at the very absurdity
of asking for a path or a way or a method. Nothing is to be done.

"A woman came up to a policeman and said, 'Oh, officer, there
is a man following me, and I think he must be crazy.'

"The officer took a good look at her. 'Yes,' he answered, 'he
must be.'"

Whenever you come to me asking for a way, I say within myself, "Here comes a crazy man again." If I don't show you the path, I look hard, unkind. If I show you the path, I mislead you.

The only thing that can be done is—you should be thrown to yourself. So I have to devise ways which are not ways, which only appear to be ways. They don't lead anywhere, because there is nowhere to go. Everybody is already there. There is nowhere to go.

I devise paths and methods just to tire you, exhaust you, so one day, in deep exhaustion, you simply drop all seeking. Exhausted, you fall down on the ground . . . tired—tired of all ways and all methods, tired of the very seeking and the search . . . and suddenly a peace descends on you—the peace which is beyond understanding. And you will laugh, because it was always possible. It was because of you that it was not descending. You were running away.

All paths lead where; truth is here. All paths lead somewhere, and truth is always here. No paths can bring you to yourself.

That's why I say try hard, so that you can be tired soon. Don't go slow. Lukewarm you can go for lives and lives, hoping and hoping. Try hard. Try absolutely, totally, so that you can be tired—so much so that the sheer tiredness drops the whole effort, and suddenly lying on the ground you become aware of the reality that is here.

God is not a thing. God is the whole performance. You cannot catch hold of it. Nirvana is not somewhere. It is the whole performance of life.

I was reading a little story:

It was springtime, and a teacher said to his little pupils, "I saw something the other day, and I wonder if any of you have seen it. If you know it, don't say what it is. I went out and saw it coming up from the ground about ten inches high, and on top of it was a little round ball of fluff, and if you went WOOF, a whole galaxy of stars flew out. Now what was it like before the little ball of stars appeared?"

One said, "It was a little yellow flower, like a sunflower, only very small."

"And what was it like before that?"

A little girl said, "It was like a tiny, green umbrella, half closed, with a yellow lining showing."

"Yes, but what was it like before that?"

One of them said, "It was a little rosette of green leaves coming out of the ground."

"Now, do you all know what it is?"

They roared back, "Dandelion!"

"And did you ever pick dandelions?" Most of them said yes, but the teacher said, "No, you cannot pick a dandelion. That is impossible. A dandelion is all these things you mentioned, and more, so whatever you picked, you got only a fragment of something or other. You can't pick a dandelion because a dandelion is not a thing. It is a process and a performance. And, you know, everything is a process and a performance—even you."

You cannot pick even a dandelion, even a small flower, in its totality because the totality is tremendous. How can you pick god? You cannot pick a small flower. God is this whole performance. All that is today is god; all that has ever been is god; all that is ever going to be is god. God is not a thing; it is a process. And so infinite and so vast—how can you seek god? It is impossible.

You can live, you can drop into this infinite ocean of godliness. And that door opens right now. There is no need to wait.

The whole Zen attitude is to bring to your notice the fact that there is no effort to be made. The Zen attitude is that of effortlessness. That is where it differs from yoga. Yoga is effort; Zen is effortlessness.

And of course, effort can lead somewhere, but it cannot lead to the ultimate. Effort can give you a better ego, more polished, more crystallized, but it cannot give you nirvana, it cannot give you god. That is beyond effort.

When all efforts cease, in that silence, in that beautiful emptiness, in that void, whatsoever is found is god.

Then what is to be done? The question naturally arises—then what to do? Understanding, more awareness, more witnessing. Watch yourself moving, living, being. Try to understand each moment that passes by you. Become a witness.

Remember, the witnessing does not mean judgement. You are not to judge that this is good and this is bad. The moment you judge, you lose the witness. If you say this is bad, you are already identified. If you say this is good, you have already slipped out of witnessing—you have become a judge.

A witness is a simple witness. You just watch as you watch the traffic on the road, or someday you lie down on the ground and you watch the clouds in the sky. You don't say this is good, that is bad; you simply don't make any judgements. You watch. You are unconcerned with what is good, what is bad. You are not trying to be moral. You are not trying any concepts . . . a pure witnessing. And out of that, more and more understanding arises, and by and by you start feeling that the ordinary life is the only life; there is no other life.

And to be ordinary is the only way to be religious. All other extraordinary things are ego trips.

Just to be ordinary is the most extraordinary thing in the world, because everybody wants to be extraordinary. Nobody wants to be ordinary. To be ordinary is the only extraordinary thing. Very rarely somebody relaxes and becomes ordinary. If you ask Zen Masters, "What do you do?" they will say, "We fetch wood from the forest, we carry water from the well. We eat when we feel hungry, we drink when we feel thirsty, we go to sleep when we feel tired. This is all."

It does not look very appealing—fetching wood, carrying water, sleeping, sitting, eating. You will say, "These are ordinary things. Everybody is doing them."

These are not ordinary things, and nobody is doing them.

When you are fetching wood, you are condemning it—you would like to be the president of some country. You don't want to be a woodcutter. You go on condemning the present for some imaginary future.

Carrying water from the well, you feel you are wasting your life. You are angry. You were not made for such ordinary things. You had come with a great destiny—to lead the whole world toward a paradise, some utopia.

These are all ego trips. These are all in states of consciousness.

Just to be ordinary . . . and then suddenly what you call trivia is no more trivia, what you call profane is no more profane. Everything becomes sacred. Carrying wood becomes sacred. Fetching water from the well becomes sacred.

And when every act becomes sacred, when every act becomes meditative and prayerful, only then are you moving deeper into life—and then life opens all the mysteries to you. Then you are becoming capable. Then you are becoming receptive. The more receptive you become, the more life becomes available.

This is my whole teaching: to be ordinary . . . to be so ordinary that the very desire to be extraordinary disappears. Only then can you be in the present; otherwise you cannot be in the present.

Montaigne has written: "We seek other conditions because we know not how to enjoy our own, and go outside of ourselves for want of knowing what it is like inside of us. So it is no use raising ourselves on stilts, for even on stilts we have to walk on our own legs, and sitting on the loftiest throne in the world we are still sitting on our behind." Wherever you are—fetching water or sitting on the throne as a king or as a president or a prime minister—makes no difference. Wherever you are, you are yourself.

If you are miserable in carrying wood, you will be miserable in being a president, because outside things can change nothing. If you are happy being a beggar, only then can you be happy being an emperor; there is no other way.

Your happiness has something to do with your quality of consciousness. It has nothing to do with outside things.

Unless you become awake, everything is going to make you more and more miserable. Once you are awake, everything brings tremendous happiness, tremendous benediction. It does not depend on anything else; it simply depends on the depth of your being, on your receptivity.

Carry wood, and when carrying wood just carry wood—and enjoy the beauty of it. Don't go on thinking of something else. Don't compare it. This moment is tremendously beautiful. This moment can become a satori. This moment can become the moment of samadhi.

Fetching water, be so totally in it that nothing is left outside. Fetching water, you are not there; only the process of fetching water is there. This is what nirvana is, enlightenment is.

I am talking to you; I am not there . . . just enjoying a chitchat with you, gossiping with you.

Listening to me, if you are also not there, then everything is fulfilled perfectly. If you are there listening to me, watching by the corner, standing there . . . watching if something valuable is being said so that you can hoard it for future use, watching if something meaningful is said so that you can make it part of your knowledge— "it will be helpful to seek something, to be something"—then you will miss me.

I am not saying anything meaningful. I am not saying anything for any purpose in view. I am not giving you some knowledge. I am not here to make you more knowledgeable.

If you can listen to me the way I am talking to you . . . this moment is total, you are not moving outside it, the future has disappeared . . . then you will have a glimpse of satori. Remember that we are engaging here in a certain activity. This activity has to be so prayerful, so meditative, that in this activity, past is no more a burden and future does not corrupt it and this moment remains pure. This moment simply remains this moment.

Then I am not here and you are not there. Then this crowd disappears. Then we become waves of one ocean—that ocean is life, that ocean is god, that ocean is nirvana.

Nirvana is such a deep relaxation of your being that you disappear in that relaxation. Tense, you are; relaxed, you are not. Your ego can only exist if you are tense. If you are relaxed, god is, you are not.

Now the story, a very simple story. All Zen stories are very simple. If you understand them, they show something. If you don't understand them then they say nothing.

All the great Masters of the world have used the parable as a medium for their message, because the parable creates a picture. It is less conceptual; it brings things more to the heart. It reveals more, says less. There is no need for the mind to intellectualize about it. The parable is there, completely clear.

Muso, the national teacher,
and one of the most illustrious masters of his day,
left the capital in the company of a disciple
for a distant province.

On reaching the Tenryu River
they had to wait for an hour
before they could board the ferry.
Just as the ferry was about to leave the shore
a drunken samurai ran up
and jumped into the packed boat,
nearly swamping it.

A drunken samurai . . . He may not be ordinarily drunk, but
a samurai is always drunk. A samurai is a man who is after power.
A samurai is a warrior. A samurai is drunk with the ego. He may
not be drunk ordinarily—that is not the point. He may have been
drunk, but all people who are after power are drunk.

The more you are after power, the more you are unconscious,
because only unconsciousness can seek power. Consciousness
lives life. Consciousness does not bother about power, because
what is the use of power?

The use of power is that you can live someday through it. First
you collect power . . . maybe it is hidden in the money, or in the
sword. First you prepare—power is a preparation—and then someday you will live.

. . . a drunken samurai ran up
and jumped into the packed boat,
nearly swamping it.
He tottered wildly as the small craft
made its way across the river.
The ferryman,
fearing for the safety of his passengers,
begged him to stand quietly.
"We're like sardines in here,"
said the samurai gruffly.
Then, pointing to Muso,
"Why not toss out the bonzae?"

"Bonzae" means a Zen priest, a Zen monk.

The story is beautiful. If politicians were allowed, then they
would not like religious people on the earth at all. They would kill

them, they would toss them out of the boat—because the only danger for the politician is the religious consciousness. The more people become religious, the more politics loses luster.

The politician is after power, and the religious man is not after anything. The religious man wants to live herenow, and the politician is always preparing for some future—future which never comes. The politician is always after some utopia, chasing it . . . after some dream. It never comes. All political revolutions have failed—failed utterly—because you go on sacrificing for the future, sacrificing the present for the future. And if the present is destroyed, from where is the future to come? It is going to be born out of the present.

You go on murdering the present in the hope that someday a beautiful future will be born out of it.

A beautiful future can be born only if the present is lived beautifully.

Politicians are always against religious people. If they are not, that simply means religious people are not religious people. Then religious people are also playing politics—in the name of religion. Christianity, Islam, Hinduism—all politics in the name of religion.

A really religious person wants to live herenow. He is not worried about the future and he is not trying to bring any revolution in the world, because he knows there is only one life and there is only one revolution and there is only one radical transformation—and that is one's own being.

He wants to love, he wants to live, he wants to pray, he wants to meditate. He wants to be left alone; nobody should disturb. He does not want to interfere in anybody's life and he does not want that anybody should be allowed to interfere in his life. And the whole politics is nothing but this—interfering in others' lives. Maybe you pretend that you are interfering for their sake . . . but you are interfering in people's lives.

The story is beautiful. Out of all persons the samurai said,

"Why not throw this bonzae out of the boat? It is much too
crowded."

"We're like sardines in here,"
said the samurai gruffly.
Then, pointing to Muso,
"Why not toss out the bonzae?"
"Please be patient,"
Muso said, "We'll reach the other side soon."

Ordinarily we should expect him to become angry, but he
simply says, Please be patient. The other shore is not very far
away.

It is a very symbolic sentence. A religious person remains
patient, because he sees, he continuously understands, that
this life is not worth being impatient about—the other shore is
continuously coming close. Nothing is worth being impatient.
Patience is more paying, gives you more of life. Becoming
impatient means you will miss this moment. You will become
restless.

He said, Don't be worried. It is a question of a few moments.
No need to throw me or anybody else out; no need to create any
conflict. The other shore is coming close. We will reach the other
side soon.

This is the whole attitude of a religious person. He is not worried about trivia. Somebody has stolen his money. He is not worried
about it; it doesn't matter. Somebody has insulted him—it does
not matter.

It matters only to people who are not living life. Then ordinary,
useless things, meaningless things, become very meaningful. A

person who is living his life totally is so happy with it he is not disturbed. Whatsoever happens on the periphery makes no difference to the center. He remains the center of the cyclone.

"What!" bawled the samurai. "Me be patient?
Listen here, if you don't jump off this thing
I swear I'll drown you."

A politician, a power-oriented person, cannot be patient. The more impatient he is, the more possibility of succeeding in the world of power and politics. He cannot be patient, because time is running fast. Only a religious person can be patient, because he has come to know the quality of eternity. Paradoxically, the religious person knows that this life is going to end, but underneath this life there is a life which never ends. Paradoxically he knows this time is going to end in death but hidden beneath this time is eternity.

If you enter life you enter eternity. If you remain on the surface you remain in time. Time is impatience.

Look. In the West people are more time-conscious and of course more impatient. In the East people are not so time-conscious; naturally they are not so impatient.

Time brings impatience.

Christians are more impatient than Hindus because Hindus have an idea of rebirth and Christians don't have any idea of rebirth. Only this life . . . such a small life, seventy years—almost one-third is lost in sleep. By the time one becomes a little aware half of the life is gone and then in small things—earning the bread making a house working for the children the wife—the life is gone. One becomes impatient.

How to live more in such a small time? The only way the West has found is to go on increasing speed—the only way. If it used to take one day to travel, travel in five minutes so that you can save time. This too great a hankering for speed is part of impatience. You can save time but then you don't know what to do with that time. You use it in saving more time . . . and this goes on and on.

Impatience is a feverish way of living. One should relax. Once you relax the time disappears and eternity reveals to you its own nature.

"What! Me be patient? Listen here, if you don't jump off this thing I swear I will drown you."

A politician can't be patient. You cannot think of Lenin or Hitler meditating. It would be a sheer wastage of time.

When you come to me from the West and you start meditating it is really a miracle. It is against all the conditioning that you have gone through. When you go back nobody will be able to understand what has happened to you . . . just wasting time— because time has to be used. It is already too short. Life is short and so many desires to be fulfilled. Why waste it in sitting with closed eyes and watching the navel? Do something before life is gone. If you live on the surface, you will remain impatient. If you enter deeper into the stream, you will come to feel that this life is not all, and the periphery is not the total. And the waves belong to the ocean, but the ocean itself is not only the waves—hidden just underneath the waves of time is the ocean of eternity.

A religious person can be patient, can be infinitely patient, be- cause he knows nothing begins and nothing ends.

The master's calm so infuriated the samurai
that he struck Muso's head with his iron fan,
drawing blood.

And it happens. If the Master had been angry, the samurai
could have understood the language—his own language—but because the Master remained silent . . . not only silent, absolutely
patient . . . this infuriated him very much.

If somebody insults you and you remain silent, as if nothing
has happened, the person will get more angry; he will get an-
grier. If you had been angry he could have understood it, but
he cannot understand the silence. In fact, in your silence he
feels very much insulted. In your silence you become a tower, a
height. In your silence he becomes like a worm, a very small
thing. That hurts.

Jesus has said, "if somebody slaps your right cheek, give him
the left also."

Nietzsche commented on this, saying, "Never do this, because
this will insult the other person more. Rather, hit him hard. He
will respect that more. At least you accept him as your equal."

And Nietzsche is also right. He has a very penetrating eye.

A religious person . . . his very presence infuriates the politician. And when he is insulted and he takes it easily, as if nothing
has happened, that drives the other person almost mad.

That's how they crucified Jesus. The priests, the politicians,
the power-addicted people, they could not tolerate this humble
and simple man. He was not doing any harm to them. In fact, he
was teaching people harmless things. He was teaching them to
become innocent like children. He was teaching them "blessed
are the meek." But they became infuriated. They had to kill him,

because his very presence became very humiliating to them. Such a tower, such a peak, a pinnacle of love, compassion, humbleness—they could not tolerate him.

Muso's disciple had had enough by this time,
and as he was a powerful man,
wanted to challenge the samurai.
"I can't permit him to go on living after this," he said.

A disciple is a disciple. He has not yet understood. He is still in the same ego. Maybe he has become religious, but the ego continues.

If somebody says something against me, you will feel angry. Now your ego is attached to me. If somebody says that this man is nothing, you become angry. Not because you are too much concerned with this man, but because if this man is nothing and you are following this man, you are even worse than nothing. It hits the ego. If you follow me I must be the greatest master in the world. You are following me—how can you follow me if I am not the greatest master in the world?

Remember, that is again a game of the ego. You will try to prove that "my master is the greatest master in the world." It is not a question of the master. How can you be a follower of a lesser master? Impossible. You—and a follower of a lesser master? That's not possible.

"I can't permit him," said the disciple, "to go on living
    after this."

"Why get so worked up over a trifle?"
Muso said with a smile.
"It's exactly in matters of this kind
that the bonzae's training proves itself.
Patience, you must remember,
is more than just a word."

It is a great experience. Now this is the moment to be patient and to enjoy it. This fellow has given a beautiful opportunity to be patient. Be thankful to him. He has given a challenge. But don't let that challenge become a challenge for your ego. Let that be a challenge for your patience. The same situation—but you can use it or you can be used by it.

If you are used by it you are an unconscious man. Then you react. All reaction is unconscious.

If you are conscious you never react. You act. Action is conscious, reaction is unconscious.

Reaction means that that man became the master of the situation: he pushed the button and you became angry. You became a puppet in his hands. But if you remain patient, if you smile, suddenly you are out of the vicious circle of unconsciousness.

Use situations and then you will come to see that even enemies are friends and even darkest nights will bring beautiful dawns. And when there was anger thrown at you, you will see compassion arising in you. These are the rarest moments. And you will feel thankful and grateful to the person who created the situation.

"Why get so worked up over a trifle?
It's exactly in matters of this kind
that the bonzae's training proves itself.

Patience, you must remember,
is more than just a word."

Patience is a great experience, a great existential experience.

Then he recited an extempore waka:
"The beater and the beaten:
mere players of a game
ephemeral as a dream."

This is what witnessing is all about.

If you can become a witness in a situation, suddenly you are out of it, no more part of it. If you lose your witnessing, even in a dream you become part of It.

You go to the movie, you watch the movie. You are just a watcher there, but sooner or later you forget all about your being a watcher—you become part of the story. You smile, you cry, you weep, you become angry, you become agitated—and there is nothing on the screen, just shadows passing, but you have lost the witnessing. You are almost identified now. You are part of the story now. Then even shadows passing on the screen become realities.

Just the opposite happens: if you stand by the side of the road and simply watch people passing, suddenly you will see real persons have become ephemeral, shadows on the screen.

The whole thing depends on you. If you are identified, an unreal thing becomes real. If you are unidentified, even a real thing becomes unreal.

A man who comes to know what witnessing is, for him this whole life is nothing but a big dream, a big drama.

"The beater and the beaten:
mere players of a game
ephemeral as a dream."

This is one of the greatest insights the East has achieved—that life, life that you know as life, is ephemeral, illusory, maya. It is not real.

There is another life. If you become aware, then you enter the temple of reality. Unawareness allows you only to live in a dream.

When the boat reached shore,
and Muso and his disciple alighted,
the samurai ran up
and prostrated himself at the master's feet.
Then and there he became a disciple.

First, if you remain silent when the situation was ordinarily demanding anger, if you remain patient when the other was expecting impatience and trouble, he will be infuriated, he will be hurt, humiliated. He would like to take revenge—you are playing god to him.

But if you continue, if you are not tempted and you remain in your silence, in your tranquility, you remain centered and rooted in your being, sooner or later the other is going to relax. Because silence is such a power, silence is such a transforming force, silence is so alchemical . . . it is the only magic in the world . . . the other is bound to be transformed.

Just wait a little. Don't be in a hurry. The other will take a little time. Give him opportunity.

The samurai ran, fell at the feet of the master.

Then and there he became a disciple.

Whenever you come against something like this—a real patience, a real substantial silence—deep down something is touched in your heart also. Deep down you are no more the same. Something real has penetrated like a ray of light into your darkness.

The world is transformed by people who live in this world as if this world is just a dream. People are changed, transfigured, by those who live in this world unconcerned, indifferent to trivia . . . who live a life of inner centering, who live in the world but don't allow the world to enter them, who live in the world but the world does not live in them, who remain untouched, who carry their silence everywhere—in the marketplace they remain in their inner temple . . . nothing distracts them from their being.

These people become catalytic agents. These people bring a totally new quality to human consciousness. A Buddha, a Jesus, a Krishna, a Mohammed—they bring another world into this world.

That is the meaning of the Hindu word "avatar." It means they bring god into the world; the god descends through them. A vision . . . they become windows. Through them you can have a vision, a glimpse of something that is beyond.

One of the most influential writers, authors, and thinkers of the West was Aldous Huxley. He was very much in tune with the Eastern idea of inner centering. He was one of the Western minds who penetrated very deeply into the Eastern attitude toward life. It is said that when a Californian brushfire destroyed a lifetime's possessions, Aldous Huxley felt only an unexpected freedom. "I feel clean," he said.

He had a really beautiful collection of rare antiques, rare books, rare paintings—a whole life's possessions—and the possessions were destroyed in a fire. Looking at the flames, he could not believe it himself that he simply felt unburdened, a sense of freedom. Disturbed not at all; on the contrary, a sense of freedom—as if the fire had been a friend. And later on he said, "I feel clean." This is the Eastern attitude.

If you are centered, nothing can be destroyed. No fire can destroy your centering. Not even death is capable of distracting you.

And this centering is possible only if you start living each moment meditatively, fully alert, aware. Don't move like an automaton. Don't react like a mechanism. Become conscious. Collect yourself more and more so that a crystallized consciousness continuously illuminates your inner being, a flame goes on burning there and it lights wherever you move. The path, the way, whatsoever you do, it lights it.

This inner flame, this inner light is there, potentially there . . . like a seed. Once you start using it, it sprouts. Soon you will see—the spring has come and it is blossoming and you are full of the fragrance of the unknown and the unknowable. God has descended in you.

Not Knowing Is the Most Intimate

*How Zen Master Hogen's aimless
pilgrimage brought him home*

On the
extraordinary
intelligence
of innocence

Ascending to the high seat, Dogen Zenji said:
"Zen Master Hogen studied with Keishin Zenji.
Once Keishin Zenji asked him, 'Joza, where do you go?'
Hogen said, 'I am making pilgrimage aimlessly.'
Keishin said, 'What is the matter of your pilgrimage?'
Hogen said, 'I don't know.'
Keishin said, 'Not knowing is the most intimate.'
Hogen suddenly attained great enlightenment."[3]

[3] Copyright © Zen Center of Los Angeles 2002. Reprinted from *On Zen Practice: Body, Breath, and Mind*, with permission of Wisdom Publications, 199 Elm Street, Somerville, MA 02144 U.S.A, www.wisdompubs.org

Zen is just Zen. There is nothing comparable to it. It is unique—unique in the sense that it is the most ordinary and yet the most extraordinary phenomenon that has happened to human consciousness. It is the most ordinary because it does not believe in knowledge, it does not believe in mind. It is not a philosophy, not a religion either. It is the acceptance of the ordinary existence with a total heart, with one's total being, not desiring some other world, supramundane, supramental. It has no interest in any esoteric nonsense, no interest in metaphysics at all. It does not hanker for the other shore; this shore is more than enough. Its acceptance of this shore is so tremendous that through that very acceptance it transforms this shore—and this very shore becomes the other shore:

> *This very body the buddha;*
> *This very earth the lotus paradise.*

Hence it is ordinary. It does not want you to create a certain kind of spirituality, a certain kind of holiness. All that it asks is that you live your life with immediacy, spontaneity. And then the mundane becomes the sacred.

The great miracle of Zen is in the transformation of the mundane into the sacred. And it is tremendously extraordinary because *this* way life has never been approached before, *this* way life has never been respected before.

Zen goes beyond Buddha and beyond Lao Tzu. It is a culmination, a transcendence, both of the Indian genius and of the Chinese genius. The Indian genius reached its highest peak in Gautam the Buddha and the Chinese genius reached its highest peak in Lao Tzu. And the meeting . . . the essence of Buddha's teaching and the essence of Lao Tzu's teaching merged into one stream so deeply that no separation is possible now. Even to make a distinction between what belongs to Buddha and what to Lao Tzu is impossible, the merger has been so total. It is not only a synthesis, it is an integration. Out of this meeting Zen was born. Zen is neither Buddhist nor Taoist and yet both.

To call Zen "Zen Buddhism" is not right because it is far more. Buddha is not so earthly as Zen is. Lao Tzu is tremendously earthly, but Zen is not only earthly: its vision transforms the earth into heaven. Lao Tzu is earthly, Buddha is unearthly, Zen is both— and in being both it has become the most extraordinary phenomenon.

The future of humanity will go closer and closer to the approach of Zen, because the meeting of the East and West is possible only through something like Zen, which is earthly and yet unearthly. The West is very earthly, the East is very unearthly. Who is going to become the bridge? Buddha cannot be the bridge; he is so essentially Eastern, the very flavor of the East, the very fragrance of the East, uncompromising. Lao Tzu cannot be the bridge; he is too earthly. China has always been very earthly. China is more part of the Western psyche than of the Eastern psyche.

It is not an accident that China is the first country in the East to turn Communist, to become materialist, to believe in a godless philosophy, to believe that man is only matter and nothing else. This is not just accidental. China has been earthly for almost five thousand years; it is very Western. Hence Lao Tzu cannot become the bridge; he is more like Zorba the Greek. Buddha is so unearthly you cannot even catch hold of him—how can he become the bridge?

When I look all around, Zen seems to be the only possibility, because in Zen, Buddha and Lao Tzu have become one. The meeting has already happened. The seed is there, the seed of that great bridge which can make East and West one. Zen is going to be the meeting point. It has a great future—a great past and a great future.

And the miracle is that Zen is neither interested in the past nor in the future. Its total interest is in the present. Maybe that's why the miracle is possible, because the past and the future are bridged by the present.

The present is not part of time. Have you ever thought about it? How long is the present? The past has a duration, the future has a duration. What is the duration of the present? How long does it last? Between the past and the future can you measure the present? It is immeasurable; it is almost not. It is not time at all: it is the penetration of eternity into time.

And Zen lives in the present. The whole teaching is: how to be in the present, how to get out of the past which is no more and how not to get involved in the future which is not yet, and just to be rooted, centered, in that which is.

The whole approach of Zen is of immediacy, but because of that it can bridge the past and the future. It can bridge many things: it can bridge the past and the future, it can bridge the East and the West, it can bridge body and soul. It can bridge the unbridgeable worlds: this world and that, the mundane and the sacred.

Before we enter into this small anecdote it will be good to understand a few things. The first: the Masters do not tell the truth. Even if they want to they cannot; it is impossible. Then what is their function? What do they go on doing? They cannot tell the truth, but they can call forth the truth which is fast asleep in you. They can provoke it, they can challenge it. They can shake you up, they can wake you up. They cannot give you God, truth, nirvana, because in the first place you already have it all with you. You are born with it. It is innate, it is intrinsic. It is your very nature. So anybody who pretends to give you the truth is simply exploiting your stupidity, your gullibility. He is cunning—cunning and utterly ignorant too. He knows nothing; not even a glimpse of truth has happened to him. He is a pseudo Master.

Truth cannot be given; it is already in you. It can be called forth, it can be provoked. A context can be created, a certain space can be created in which it rises in you and is no more asleep, becomes awakened.

The function of the Master is far more complex than you think. It would have been far easier, simpler, if truth could be conveyed. It cannot be conveyed, hence indirect ways and means have to be devised.

The New Testament has the beautiful story of Lazarus. Christians have missed the whole point of it. Christ is so unfortunate— he has fallen into the wrong company. Not even a single Christian theologian has been able to discover the meaning of the story of Lazarus, his death and resurrection.

Lazarus dies. He is the brother of Mary Magdalene and Martha and a great devotee of Jesus. Jesus is far away; by the time he gets the information and the invitation, "Come immediately," two days have already passed, and by the time he reaches Lazarus' place four days have passed. But Mary and Martha are waiting for him— their trust is such. The whole village is laughing at them. They are being stupid in others' eyes because they are keeping the corpse in a cave; they are watching day in, day out, guarding the corpse. The corpse has already started stinking; it is deteriorating.

The village people are saying, "You are fools! Jesus cannot do anything. When somebody is dead, somebody is dead!"

Jesus comes. He goes to the cave—he does not enter into the cave—he stands outside and calls Lazarus forth. The people have gathered. They must be laughing: "This man seems to be crazy!"

Somebody says to him, "What are you doing? He is dead! He has been dead for four days. In fact, to enter into the cave is difficult—his body is stinking. It is impossible! Whom are you calling?"

But, unperturbed, Jesus shouts again and again, "Lazarus, come out!"

And the crowd is in for a great surprise: Lazarus walks out of the cave—shaken, shocked, as if out of a great slumber, as if he had fallen into a coma. He himself cannot believe what has happened, why he is in the cave.

This in fact is just a way of saying what the function of a Master

is. Whether Lazarus was really dead or not is not the point.
Whether Jesus was capable of raising the dead or not is not the
point. To get involved in those stupid questions is absurd. Only
scholars can be so foolish. No man of understanding will think
that this is something historical. It is far more! It is not a fact, it is
a truth. It is not something that happens in time, it is something
more: something that happens in eternity.

You are all dead. You are all in the same situation as Lazarus.
You are all living in your dark caves. You are all stinking and deteriorating . . . because death is not something that comes one day
suddenly—you are dying every day. Since the day of your birth you
have been dying. It is a long process; it takes seventy, eighty,
ninety years to complete it. *Each moment* something of you dies,
something in you dies, but you are absolutely unaware of the
whole situation. You go on as if you are alive; you go on living as if
you know what life is.

The function of the Master is to call forth: "Lazarus, come out
of the cave! Come out of your grave! Come out of your death!"

The Master cannot give you the truth but he can call forth the
truth. He can stir something in you. He can trigger a process in
you which will ignite a fire, a flame. Truth you are—just so much
dust has gathered around you. The function of the Master is negative: he has to give you a bath, a shower, so the dust disappears.

That's exactly the meaning of Christian baptism. That's what
John the Baptist was doing in the river Jordan. But people go on
misunderstanding. Today also baptism happens in the churches;
it is meaningless.

John the Baptist was preparing people for an inner bath. When
they were ready he would take them symbolically into the river
Jordan. That was only symbolic—symbolizing that the Master can
give you a bath. He can take the dust, the dust of centuries, away
from you. And suddenly all is clear, all is clarity. That clarity is enlightenment.

The great Master Daie says: "All the teachings of the sages, of the saints, of the masters, have expounded no more than this: they are commentaries on your sudden cry, 'Ah, This!' "

When suddenly you are clear and a great joy and rejoicing arises in you, and your whole being, every fiber of your body, mind, and soul dances, and you say, "Ah, this! Alleluia!" a great shout of joy arises in your being, that is enlightenment. Suddenly stars come down from the rafters. You become part of the eternal dance of existence.

In "Death's Echo," Auden says:

Dance till the stars come down from the rafters!
Dance, dance, dance till you drop!

Yes, it happens—it is not something that you have to do. It is something that even if you want not to do, you will find it impossible; you will find it impossible to resist. You will have to dance.

The beauty of this, the beauty of now, the joy that existence is and the closeness of it . . . Yes, stars come down from the rafters. They are so close you can just touch them; you can hold them in your hands.

Daie is right. He says:

All the teachings the sages expounded are no more than com-
mentaries on your sudden cry, "AH, THIS!"

The whole heart saying, "Aha!" And the silence that follows it, and the peace, and the joy, and the meeting, and the merger, and the orgasmic experience, the ecstasy . . . !

Masters don't teach the truth; there is no way to teach it. It is a transmission beyond scriptures, beyond words. It is a transmission. It is energy provoking energy in you. It is a kind of synchronicity.

The Master has disappeared as an ego; he is pure joy. And the disciple sits by the side of the Master slowly slowly partaking of

his joy, of his being, eating and drinking out of that eternal, inex-
haustible source: *Ais Dhammo Sanantano*. And one day . . . and
one cannot predict when that day will come; it is unpredictable.
One day suddenly it has happened: a process has started in you
which reveals the truth of your being to you. You come face to face
with yourself. God is not somewhere else: he is now, here.

The Masters illuminate and confirm realization. They illuminate in a thousand and one ways. They go on pointing toward the
truth: fingers pointing to the moon. But there are many fools who
start clinging to the fingers. By clinging to the fingers you will not
see the moon, remember. There are even greater fools who start
biting the fingers. That is not going to give you any nourishment.
Forget the finger and look at where it is pointing.

The Masters illuminate. They shower great light—they are
light—they shower great light on your being. They are like a
searchlight: they focus their being on your being. You have lived in
darkness for centuries, for millions of lives. Suddenly a Master's
searchlight starts revealing a few forgotten territories in you. They
are within you; the Master is not bringing them—he is simply
bringing his light, he is focusing himself on you. And the Master
can focus only when the disciple is open, when the disciple is surrendered, when the disciple is ready to learn, not to argue, when
the disciple has come not to accumulate knowledge but to know
truth, when the disciple is not only curious but is a seeker and is
ready to risk all. Even if life has to be risked and sacrificed the disciple is ready. In fact, when you risk your sleepy life, you sacrifice
your sleepy life, you attain to a totally different quality of life: the
life of light, of love, the life which is beyond death, beyond time,
beyond change.

They illuminate and confirm realization. First the Master illuminates the way, the truth that is within you. And secondly: when
you realize it, when you recognize it . . . It is very difficult for you
to believe that you have attained it. The most unbelievable thing is
when realization of truth happens to you, because you have been

told that it is very difficult, almost impossible, and that it takes millions of lives to arrive at it. And you have been told it is somewhere else—maybe in heaven—and when you recognize it within yourself, how can you believe it?

The Master confirms it. He says, "Yes, this is it!" His confirmation is as much needed as his illumination. He begins by illuminating and ends by confirming. The Masters are evidence of truth, not its proof.

Meditate over the subtle difference between evidence and proof. The Master is an evidence; he is a witness. He has seen, he has known, he has become. You can feel it; the evidence can be felt. You can come closer and closer; you can allow the fragrance of the Master to penetrate to the innermost core of your being. The Master is only evidence; he is not proof. If you want any proof . . . there is no proof.

God can neither be proved nor disproved; it is not an argument. God is not a hypothesis, it is not a theory: it is experience. The Master is living evidence. But to see it you will need a different approach than you are accustomed to.

You know how to approach a teacher, how to approach a professor, how to approach a priest. They don't require much because they simply impart information which can be done even by a tape recorder or by a computer or by a gramophone record or by a book.

I was a student in a university. I never attended the classes of my professors. Naturally, they were offended. And one day the head of the department called me and he said, "Why have you joined the university? We never see you, you never attend any classes. And remember: when the examination time comes, don't ask for an attendance record—because seventy-five percent attendance is a must to enter into the examination."

I took hold of the hand of that old man and I said, "You come with me—I will show you where I am and why I have entered the university."

He was a little afraid of where I was taking him and why. And it was a well-known fact that I was a little eccentric! He said, "But where are you taking me?"

I said, "I will show you that you have to give me one hundred percent attendance. You come with me."

I took him to the library and I told the librarian, "You tell this old man—has there ever been a single day when I have not been in the library?"

The librarian said, "Even on holidays he has been here. If the library is not open then this student goes on sitting in the garden of the library, but he comes. And every day we have to tell him, 'Now please, you leave, because it is closing time.'"

I told the professor, "I find the books far more clear than your so-called professors. And, moreover, they simply repeat what is already written in the books, so what is the point of going on listening to them secondhand? I can look in the books directly!"

I told him, "If you can prove that your teachers are teaching something which is not in the books, then I am ready to come to the classes. If you cannot prove it, then keep it in mind that you have to give me one hundred percent attendance—otherwise I will create trouble!"

And I never went to ask him; he gave me one hundred percent attendance. He followed the point; it was so simple. He said, "You are right. Why listen to secondhand knowledge? You can go directly to the books. I know those professors—I myself am just a gramophone record. The truth is," he said to me, "that for thirty years I have not read anything. I just go on using my old notes."

For thirty years he has been teaching the same thing again and again and again; and in thirty years' time, millions of books have been published.

You know how to approach a teacher, you know how to approach a book, you know how to approach dead information, but you don't know how to approach a Master. It is a totally different way of communing. It is not communication, it is communion— because the Master is not a proof but an evidence. He is not an argument for God, he is a witness for God. He does not possess great knowledge about God, he knows. He is not knowledgeable, he simply knows.

Remember, to know *about* is worthless. The word "about" means around. To know about something means to go on moving in circles, around and around. The word "about" is beautiful. Whenever you read "about," read "around." When somebody says, "I know *about* God," read: he knows *around* God. He goes in a circle. And real knowing is never about, never around; it is direct, it is a straight line.

Jesus says: "Straight is the path . . ." It does not go in circles; it is a jump from the periphery to the center. The Master is an evidence of that jump, that quantum leap, that transformation.

You have to approach the Master with great love, with great trust, with an open heart. You are not aware who you are. He is aware who he is, he is aware who you are. The caterpillar might be said to be unaware that it may become a butterfly. You are caterpillars—Bodhisattvas. All caterpillars are Bodhisattvas and all Bodhisattvas are caterpillars. A Bodhisattva means one who can become a butterfly, who can become a Buddha, who is a Buddha in the seed, in essence. But how can the caterpillar be aware that he can become a butterfly? The only way is to commune with butterflies, to see butterflies moving in the wind, in the sun. Seeing them soaring high, seeing them moving from one flower to another flower, seeing their beauty, their color, maybe a deep desire, a longing, arises in the caterpillar: "Can I also be the same?" In that very moment the caterpillar has started awakening, a process has been triggered.

The Master/disciple relationship is the relationship between a caterpillar and a butterfly, a friendship between a caterpillar and a butterfly. The butterfly cannot prove that the caterpillar can become a butterfly; there is no logical way. But the butterfly can provoke a longing in the caterpillar—that is possible.

The Master helps you to reach your own experience. He does not give you the Vedas, the Koran, the Bible; he throws you to yourself. He makes you aware of your inner sources. He makes you aware of your own juice, of your own godliness. He liberates you from the scriptures. He liberates you from the interpretations of others. He liberates you from all belief. He liberates you from all speculation, from all guesswork. He liberates you from philosophy and from religion and from theology. He liberates you, in short, from the world of words—because the word is the problem.

You become so much obsessed with the word "love" that you forget that love is an experience, not a word. You become so obsessed with the word "God" that you forget that God is an experience, not a word. The word "God" is not God, and the word "fire" is not fire, and the word "love" is not love either.

The Master liberates you from words, he liberates you from all kinds of imaginative philosophies. He brings you to a state of wordless silence. The failure of religion and philosophy is that they all become substitutes for real experience. Beware of it!

Marlene and Florence, two Denver secretaries, were chatting over lunch.

"I was raped last night by a scholar," whispered Marlene.

"Really?" said Florence. "How did you know he was a scholar?"

"I had to help him."

Scholars are crippled people, paralyzed, hung up in their heads. They have forgotten everything except words. They are great system-makers. They accumulate beautiful theories; they arrange them in beautiful patterns, but that's all they do. They know nothing—although they deceive others and deceive themselves, too, that they know.

A man went into a restaurant to have some lunch and when the waiter came he said, "I will have a plate of kiddlies, please."

"What?" said the waiter.

"Kiddlies," said the man.

"What?" said the waiter again.

So the man picked up the menu and pointed at what he wanted. "Kiddlies," he repeated firmly.

"Ah," said the waiter. "I see. Kidneys. Why didn't you say so?"

"But," said the man, "I said kiddlies, diddle I?"

It is very difficult to pull them out. They live in their own words. They have forgotten that reality has anything else in it but words. They are utterly deaf, utterly blind. They can't see, they can't hear, they can't feel. Words are words. You can't see them, you can't feel them, but they can give you great ego.

A cannibal rushed into his village to spread the word that a hunting party had captured a Christian theologian.

"Good," said one of the cannibals enthusiastically, "I have always wanted to try a baloney sandwich."

Beware of getting lost in philosophy and religion if you really want to know what truth is. Beware of being Christian, Hindu, Mohammedan, because they are all ways of being deaf, blind, insensitive.

Three deaf British gentlemen were traveling on a train bound for London.

The first said, "Pardon me, conductor, what station is this?"

"Wembley, sir," answered the conductor.

"Good Lord!" exclaimed the second Englishman. "I am sure it is Thursday."

"So am I," agreed the third. "Let us all go into the bar car and have a drink."

That's how it goes on between professors, philosophers, theologians. They can't hear what is being said. They have their own ideas and they are so full of them, so many thick layers of words, that reality cannot reach them.

Zen says: If you can drop philosophizing, there is a hope for you. The moment you drop philosophizing you become innocent like a child. But remember: the Zen emphasis on not knowing does not mean that it emphasizes ignorance. Not knowing is not ignorance; not knowing is a state of innocence. There is neither knowledge nor ignorance; both have been transcended.

An ignorant man is one who ignores; that's how the word comes. The root is "ignoring." The ignorant person is one who goes on ignoring something essential. In that way the knowledgeable person is the most ignorant person, because he knows about heaven and hell and he knows nothing about himself. He knows about God, but he knows nothing about who he is, what this consciousness inside is. He is ignorant because he is ignoring the *most* fundamental thing in life: he is ignoring himself. He is keeping himself occupied with the nonessential. He is ignorant—full of knowledge, yet utterly ignorant.

Not knowing simply means a state of no-mind. Mind can be knowledgeable, mind can be ignorant. If you have little information you will be thought ignorant; if you have more information you will be thought knowledgeable. Between ignorance and knowledge the difference is that of quantity, of degrees. The ignorant person is less knowledgeable, that's all; the very knowledgeable person may appear to the world as less ignorant, but they are not different, their qualities are not different.

Zen emphasizes the state of not knowing. Not knowing means one is neither ignorant nor knowledgeable. One is not knowledgeable because one is not interested in mere information, and one is not ignorant because one is not ignoring—one is not ignoring the most essential quest. One is not ignoring one's own being, one's own consciousness.

Not knowing has a beauty of its own, a purity. It is just like a pure mirror, a lake utterly silent, reflecting the stars and the trees on the bank. The state of not knowing is the highest point in man's evolution.

Knowledge is introduced to the mind after physical birth. Knowing is always present, like the heart knowing how to beat or a seed knowing how to sprout, or a flower knowing how to grow, or a fish knowing how to swim. And it is quite different from knowing about things. So please make a distinction between knowledge and knowing.

The state of not knowing is really the state of knowing because when all knowledge and all ignorance have disappeared you can reflect existence as it is. Knowledge is acquired after your birth, but knowing comes with you. And the more knowledge you acquire, the more and more knowing starts disappearing because it becomes covered with knowledge. Knowledge is exactly like dust and knowing is like a mirror.

The heart of knowing is now. Knowledge is always of the past. Knowledge means memory. Knowledge means you have known something, you have experienced something, and you have accumulated your experience. Knowing is of the present. And how can you be in the present if you are clinging too much to knowledge? That is impossible; you will have to drop clinging to knowledge. And knowledge is acquired; knowing is your nature. Knowing is always now—the heart of knowing is now. And the heart of now . . . ?

The word "now" is beautiful. The heart of it is the letter O which is also a symbol for zero. The heart of now is zero, nothingness. When the mind is no more, when you are just a nothingness, just a zero—Buddha calls it exactly that, *shunya*, the zero—then everything that surrounds you, *all* that is within and without, is known. But known not as knowledge, known in a totally different way. The same way that the flower knows how to open, and the fish knows how to swim, and the child knows in the mother's womb how to grow. And you know how to breathe—even while asleep, even in a coma, you go on breathing—and the heart knows how to beat. This is a totally different kind of knowing, so intrinsic, so internal. It is not acquired, it is natural.

Knowledge is got in exchange for knowing. And when you have got knowledge, what happens to knowing? You forget knowing. You have got knowledge and you have forgotten knowing. And knowing is the door to the divine; knowledge is a barrier to the divine. Knowledge has utility in the world. Yes, it will make you more efficient, skillful, a good mechanic, this and that; you may be able to earn in a better way. All that is there and I am not denying it. And you can use knowledge in that way; but don't let knowledge become a barrier to the divine. Whenever knowledge is not needed, put it aside and drown yourself into a state of not knowing—which is also a state of knowing, real knowing. Knowledge is got in exchange for knowing and knowing is forgotten. It has only to be remembered—you have forgotten it.

The function of the Master is to help you RE-member it. The mind has to be RE-minded, for knowing is nothing but RE-cognition, RE-collection, RE-membrance. When you come across some truth, when you come across a Master, and you see the truth of his being, something within you immediately recognizes it. Not even a single moment is lost. You don't think about it, whether it is true or not—thinking needs time. When you listen to the truth, when you feel the presence of truth, when you come into close communion with the truth, something within you immediately recognizes it, with no argumentation. Not that you accept, not that you believe: you recognize. And it could not be recognized if it were not already known somehow, somewhere, deep down within you.

This is the fundamental approach of Zen.

"Has your baby brother learned to talk yet?"
"Oh, sure," replied little Mike. "Now Mummy and Daddy are
teaching him to keep quiet."

The society teaches you knowledge. So many schools, colleges, universities . . . they are all devoted to creating knowledge, more knowledge, implanting knowledge in people. And the function of the Master is just the opposite: what your society has done to you the Master has to undo. His function is basically antisocial, and nothing can be done about it. The Master is bound to be antisocial.

Jesus, Pythagoras, Buddha, Lao Tzu, they are all antisocial. Not that they want to be antisocial, but the moment they recognize the beauty of not knowing, the vastness of not knowing, the innocence of not knowing, the moment the taste of not knowing happens to them, they want to impart it to others, they want to share it with others. And that very process is antisocial.

People ask me why the society is against me. The society is *not* against me—I am antisocial. But I can't help it—I have to do my thing. I have to share what has happened to me, and in that very sharing I go against the society. Its whole structure is rooted in knowledge, and the Master's function is to destroy both knowledge and ignorance and to bring you back your childhood.

Jesus says: unless you are like small children you will not enter into the kingdom of God.

The society, in fact, makes you uprooted from your nature. It pushes you off your center. It makes you neurotic.

Conducting a university course, a famous psychiatrist was asked by a student, "Sir, you have told us about the abnormal person and his behavior, but what about the normal person?"

"When we find him," replied the psychiatrist, "we cure him."

The society goes on curing normal people. Every child is born normal, remember; then the society cures him. Then he becomes abnormal. He becomes Hindu, Mohammedan, Christian, Communist, Catholic . . . there are so many kinds of neurosis in the world. You can choose, you can shop for whatever kind of neurosis you want. Society creates all kinds; all sizes and shapes of neurosis are available, to everybody's liking.

Zen cures you of your abnormality. It makes you again normal, it makes you again ordinary. It does not make you a saint, remember. It does not make you a holy person, remember. It simply makes you an ordinary person—takes you back to your nature, back to your source.

This beautiful anecdote:

Ascending to the high seat, Dogen Zenji said: "Zen Master Hogen studied with Keishin Zenji.
Once Keishin Zenji asked him, 'Joza, where do you go?'
Hogen said, 'I am making pilgrimage aimlessly.'
Keishin said, 'What is the matter of your pilgrimage?'
Hogen said, 'I don't know.'
Keishin said, 'Not knowing is the most intimate.'
Hogen suddenly attained great enlightenment."

Now meditate over each word of this small anecdote; it contains all the great scriptures of the world. It contains more than all the great scriptures contain—because it also contains not knowing.

Ascending to the high seat . . .

This is just a symbolic, metaphorical way of saying something very significant. Zen says that man is a ladder. The lowest rung is the mind and the highest rung of the ladder is the no-mind. Zen says only people who have attained to no-mind are worthy enough to ascend to the high seat and speak to people—not everybody. It is not a question of a priest or a preacher.

Christians train preachers; they have theological colleges where preachers are trained. What kind of foolishness is this? Yes, you can teach them the art of eloquence; you can teach them how to begin a speech, how to end a speech. And that's exactly what is being taught in Christian theological colleges. Even what gestures to make, when to make a pause, when to speak slowly and when to become loud—everything is cultivated. And these stupid people go on preaching about Jesus, and they have not asked a single question!

Once I visited a theological college. The principal was my friend; he invited me. I asked him, "Can you tell me in what theological college Jesus learned? Because the Sermon on the Mount is so beautiful, he must have learned in some theological college. In what theological college did Buddha learn?"

Mohammed was absolutely uneducated, but the way he speaks, the way he sings in the Koran, is superb. It is coming from somewhere else. It is not education, it is not knowledge. It is coming from a state of no-mind.

Little Johnny was the son of the local minister. One day his teacher was asking the class what they wanted to be when they grew up.

When it was his turn to answer he replied, "I want to be a minister just like my father."

The teacher was impressed with his determination and so she asked him why he wanted to be a preacher.

"Well," he said thoughtfully, "since I have to go to church on Sunday anyway, I figure it would be more interesting to be the

*guy who stands up and yells than the one who has to sit down
and listen."*

You can create preachers, but you cannot create Masters.

In India, the seat from where a Master speaks is called *vyaspeetha*.
Vyasa was one of the greatest Masters India has ever produced,
one of the ancientmost Buddhas. He was so influential, his impact
was so tremendous, that thousands of books exist in his name
which were not written by him. But his name became so important
that anybody who wanted to sell his book would put Vyasa's name
on it instead of putting his own name. His name was guarantee
enough that the book was valuable. Now scholars go crazy deciding
which is the real book written by Vyasa.

The seat from where a Buddha speaks is called *vyaspeetha*—the
seat of the Buddha. Nobody else is allowed to ascend to the seat
unless he has attained to no-mind. "Ascending to the high seat"
is a metaphor: it says the man has attained to the state of no-
mind, he has attained the state of not-knowing which is true
knowing.

. . . Dogen Zenji said: "Zen Master Hogen studied with
    Keishin Zenji.
Once Keishin Zenji asked him, 'Joza, where do you go?' "

This is a Zen way of saying, "What is your goal in life? Where
are you going?" It also implies another question: "From where are
you coming? What is the source of your life?" It also implies,
"Who are you?"—because if you can answer where you are coming
from and where you are going to, that means you must know who
you are.

The three most important questions are: Who am I? From where do I come? and To where am I going?

. . . Keishin Zenji asked him, "Joza, where do you go?"
Hogen said, "I am making pilgrimage aimlessly."

See the beauty of the answer. This is how tremendously beautiful things transpire between a Master and a disciple. He said:

"I am making pilgrimage aimlessly."

If you are going to Kaaba, then it is not a pilgrimage because there is an aim in it; if you are going to Jerusalem or to Kashi it is not a pilgrimage. Wherever there is a goal there is ambition, and wherever there is ambition there is mind, desire. And with desire there is no possibility of any pilgrimage.

A pilgrimage can only be aimless. See the beauty of it! Only a Zen Master can approve it and only a Zen disciple can say something so tremendously revolutionary.

"I am making pilgrimage aimlessly."

The Master asks, "Where are you going?" And the disciple says, "Nowhere in particular." Aimlessly, just like a dry leaf in the wind, wherever the wind takes it: to the north, then the north is beautiful; to the south, then the south is beautiful—because all is divine. Wherever you go you encounter him. There is no need to have any aim.

The moment you have any aim you become tense; you become concentrated on the aim. The moment you have any aim you are separate from the whole. You have a private goal, and to have a private goal is the root of all ego. Not to have a private goal is to be one with the whole, and to be one with the whole is possible only if you are aimlessly wandering.

A Zen person is a wanderer, aimless, with no goal, with no future. Moment to moment he lives without any mind; just like the dry leaf he makes himself available to the winds. He says to the winds, "Take me wherever you want." If he rises on the winds high in the sky he does not feel superior to others who are lying down on the ground. If he falls to the ground he does not feel inferior to others who are rising on the wind high in the sky. He cannot fail. He cannot ever be frustrated. When there is no goal, how can you fail? And when you are not going anywhere in particular, how can you be in frustration? Expectation brings frustration. Private ambitions bring failures.

The Zen person is always victorious, even in his failure.

Keishin said, "What is the matter of your pilgrimage?"

He asks again to make certain, because he may be simply repeating. He may have read in some old Zen scriptures that "one should be aimless. When one is aimless, life is a pilgrimage." Hence the Master asks again:

. . . "What is the matter of your pilgrimage?"
Hogen said, "I don't know."

Now, if Hogen was only repeating some knowledge gathered
from scriptures or others, he would have again answered the
same thing, maybe paraphrased in a different way. He would have
been like a parrot. The Master is asking the same question, but
the answer has changed, totally changed. He simply says: I don't
know.

How can you know if you are aimless? How can you know when
you don't have any goal? How can you be when there is no goal?
The ego can exist only with goals, ambitions, desires.

Hogen said, "I don't know."

His answer, his response, is not parrotlike. He has not repeated
the same thing again. The question was the same, remember, but
the answer has changed. That's the difference between a knowledgeable person and a man of knowing, the wise man, who functions out of a state of not-knowing.

"I don't know."

Keishin must have been tremendously happy. He said:

"Not knowing is the most intimate."

Knowledge creates a distance between you and reality. The more you know, the greater is the distance—so many books between you and reality. If you have crammed the whole of the *Encyclopedia Britannica*, then there is so much distance between you and reality. Unless reality tries to find you through the jungle of the *Encyclopedia Britannica* or you try to find reality through the jungle of the *Encyclopedia Britannica*, there is not going to be any meeting. The more you know, the greater is the distance; the less you know, the thinner is the distance. If you don't know at all there is no distance at all. Then you are face to face with reality; not even face to face—*you are it*. That's why the Master said:

"Not knowing is the most intimate."

Remember, such a beautiful sutra, so exquisite, so tremendously significant:

"Not knowing is the most intimate."

The moment you don't know, intimacy arises between you and reality, a great friendship arises. It becomes a love affair. You are embracing reality; reality penetrates you, as lovers penetrate each other. You melt into it like snow melting in the sun. You become one with it. There is nothing to divide. It is knowledge that divides; it is not-knowing that unites.

Listen to this tremendously significant sutra:

"Not knowing is the most intimate." Hogen suddenly attained great enlightenment.

He must have been very close, obviously. When he said, "I don't know," he must have been just on the borderline. When he said, "I am making pilgrimage aimlessly," he was just one step away from the borderline. When he said, "I don't know," even that one step disappeared. He was standing on the borderline.

And when the Master said, when the Master confirmed, illuminated, and said, "Not knowing is the most intimate" . . . when the Master patted him on the back: "Not knowing is the most intimate" . . .

Hogen suddenly attained great enlightenment.

Immediately, that very moment, he crossed the border. Immediately his last clinging disappeared. Now he cannot even say, "I don't know."

The stupid person says, "I know"; the intelligent person comes to know that "I don't know." But there is a transcendence of both when only silence prevails. Nothing can be said, nothing can be uttered. Hogen entered that silence, that great enlightenment, and suddenly, immediately, without any lapse of time.

Enlightenment is always sudden because it is not an achievement; it is already the case. It is only a remembering, it is only a reminding, it is only a recognition. You are already enlightened; you are just not aware of it. It is awareness of that which is already the case.

Meditate over this beautiful anecdote. Let this sutra resound in your being:

"Not knowing is the most intimate."

And one never knows: sudden enlightenment may happen to you as it happened to Hogen. It is going to happen to many people here, because what I am doing every day is destroying your knowledge, destroying and destroying all your clingings and strategies of the mind. Any day when your mind collapses, when you cannot hold it together any more, there is bound to be sudden enlightenment. It is not an attainment, hence it can happen in a single moment, instantly. Society has forced you to forget it; my work is to help you remember it.

Enough for today.

Take No Notice

*The story of a housewife's
sudden enlightenment*

On the
reasons
why "self-
improvement"
often fails

The ancients said:

"(Self-)cultivation takes an unimaginable time (while)
    enlightenment in an instant is attained."
If the training is efficient, enlightenment will be attained
    in one fingersnap.
In days gone by, Ch'an Master Hui Chueh of Lang Yeh
    Mountain had a disciple who called on him for
    instruction.
The master taught her to examine into the sentence: "Take no
    notice."
She followed his instruction strictly without backsliding.
One day her house caught fire, but she said: "Take no notice."

Another day, her son fell into the water and when a bystander
called her, she said: "Take no notice."
She observed exactly her master's instruction by laying down
all casual thoughts.
One day, as her husband lit the fire to make fritters of twisted
dough, she threw into the pan full of boiling (vegetable)
oil a batter which made a noise.
Upon hearing the noise, she was instantly enlightened. Then
she threw the pan of oil on the ground, clapped her hands
and laughed.
Thinking she was insane, her husband scolded her and said:
"Why do you do this? Are you mad?"
She replied: "Take no notice."
Then she went to the Master Hui Chueh and asked him to
verify her achievement.
The master confirmed that she had obtained the holy fruit.[4]

There are two paths to the ultimate truth. The first is of self-
cultivation and the second is of enlightenment. The first is basically wrong. It only appears to be a path; it is not. One goes on and
on in circles, but one never arrives. The second does not appear
to be a path because there is no space for a path when something
happens instantly, when something happens immediately. When
something happens without taking any time, how can there be
a path?

This paradox has to be understood as deeply as possible: the
first appears to be the path but is not; the second appears not to
be a path but is. The first appears to be a path because there is infinite time; it is a time phenomenon. But anything happening in

[4] From *Ch'an and Zen Teaching* by K'uan Yü Lu (Rider, 1960). Reprinted by kind permission of author's son, Luk Wing Shiu.

time cannot lead you beyond time; anything happening in time only strengthens time.

Time means mind. Time *is* a projection of mind. It does not exist; it is only an illusion. Only the present exists—and the present is not part of time. The present is part of eternity. Past is time, future is time; both are nonexistential. The past is only memory and the future is only imagination; memory and imagination, both are nonexistential. We create the past because we cling to memory; clinging to the memory is the source of the past. And we create the future because we have so many desires yet to be fulfilled, we have so many imaginations yet to be realized. And desires need a future like a screen onto which they can be projected.

Past and future are mind phenomena; and past and future make your whole idea of time. Ordinarily you think that time is divided into three divisions: past, present, and future. That is totally wrong. That is not how the awakened ones have seen time. They say time consists only of two divisions: past and future. The present is not part of time at all; the present belongs to the beyond.

The first path—the path of self-cultivation—is a time path; it has nothing to do with eternity. And truth is eternity.

The second path—the path of enlightenment, Zen Masters have always called "the pathless path" because it does not appear to be a path at all. It cannot appear as a path, but just for the purposes of communication we will call it "the second path," arbitrarily. The second path is not part of time, it is part of eternity. Hence it happens instantaneously; it happens in the present. You cannot desire it, you cannot be ambitious for it.

On the first path, the false path, all is allowed. You can imagine, you can desire, you can be ambitious. You can change all your worldly desires into otherworldly desires. That's what the so-called religious people go on doing. They don't desire money any more—they are fed up with it, tired of it, frustrated with it, bored with it—but they start desiring God. Desire persists; it changes its object. Money is no more the object of desire but God; pleasure is no more the object of desire but bliss. But what bliss can you imagine? Whatsoever you imagine in the name of bliss is nothing but your idea of pleasure—maybe a little bit refined, cultivated, sophisticated, but it can't be more than that.

The people who stop desiring worldly things start desiring heaven and heavenly pleasures. But what are they? Magnified forms of the same old desires, in fact more dangerous than the worldly desires, because with the worldly desires one thing is absolutely certain: you are bound to get frustrated sooner or later. You will get out of them; you cannot remain in them forever. The very nature of them is such that they promise you, but they never fulfill their promises—the goods are never delivered. How long can you remain deceived by them? Even the most stupid person has glimpses, once in a while, that he is chasing illusions which cannot be fulfilled by the very nature of existence. The intelligent one comes to the realization sooner.

But with the otherworldly desires there is far greater danger because they are otherworldly, and to see them and to experience them you will have to wait till death. They will happen only after death so you cannot be free of them in life, while you are alive. And a man who has lived unconsciously his whole life, his death is going to be the culmination of unconsciousness; he will die in unconsciousness. In death also he will not be able to disillusion himself. And the person who dies in unconsciousness is born again in unconsciousness. It is a vicious circle; it goes on and on. And the person who is born in unconsciousness will repeat the same stupidities that he has been repeating for millions of lives.

Unless you become alert and aware *in* life, unless you change the quality of your living, you will not die consciously. And only a conscious death can bring you to a conscious birth; and then a far more conscious life opens its doors.

Changing worldly desires into otherworldly desires is the last strategy of the mind to keep you captive, to keep you a prisoner, to keep you in bondage.

So the first path is not really a path but a deception—but a very alluring deception. In the first place, it is *self*-cultivation. It is not against the ego; it is rooted in the refinement of the ego. Refine your ego of all grossness, then you become a self. The ego is like a raw diamond: you go on cutting it and polishing it and then it becomes a Kohinoor, very precious. That is your idea of "self," but it is nothing but ego with a beautiful name, with a spiritual flavor thrown in. It is the same old illusory ego.

The very idea that "I am" is wrong. The whole is, God is—I am not. Either I can exist or God can exist; we cannot both exist together—because if I exist, then I am a separate entity. Then I have my own existence independent of God. But God simply means the total, the whole. *How* can I be independent of it? How can I be separate from it? If I exist, I destroy the very idea of totality.

The people who deny God are the most egoistic people. It is not an accident that Friedrich Nietzsche declared God dead. He was one of the most egoistic persons possible. It was his ego that made him insane finally. Ego is insanity, the basic insanity, the most fundamental, out of which all other insanities arise. He said: "God is dead and man is free." That sentence is significant. In one sentence he has said the whole thing: man can be free only if God is dead; if God is alive, then man cannot be free, in fact man cannot exist.

The very idea that "I am" is unspiritual. The idea of the self is unspiritual.

And what is self-cultivation? It is an effort to polish; it is an effort to create a beautiful character, to drop all that is unrespectable and to create all that is respectable. That's why in different countries different things are cultivated by the spiritual people—the so-called spiritual. It depends on the society; what the society respects, that will be cultivated.

In imperial Russia, before the revolution, there was a Christian sect which believed that sexual organs should be cut, only then are you real Christians. The statement of Jesus was taken literally. Jesus has said: be eunuchs of God. And these fools followed it literally.

Every year they would gather in thousands and in a mad frenzy they would cut their sexual organs. Men would cut their genital organs, women would cut their breasts. And those who were able to do it were thought to be saints; they were very much respected—they had made a great sacrifice. Now, anywhere else they would have been thought utterly insane; but because in that particular society it was respected, they were saints.

In India you can find many people lying down on beds of thorns or needles, and they are thought to be great sages. If you look into their eyes, they are just stupid people. Lying down on a bed of thorns can't make one spiritual. It will simply deaden your body, your sensitivity. Your body will become more and more dull; it will not feel.

That's how it happens. Your face does not feel the cold because it remains open; it becomes insensitive to the cold. Your hands don't feel the cold so much because they are open; they become insensitive to the cold. Exactly in the same way you can live naked. Only for the beginning few months will you feel the cold; slowly slowly your body will adjust.

That's how the Jaina monks live naked. And their followers praise them like anything; they think: "This is what real spirituality is. Look, they have gone beyond the body!" They have gone nowhere; the body has just become dull. And when the body becomes dull it naturally creates a dullness of the mind too, because body and mind are deeply one. The body is the outer shell of the mind and the mind is the inner core of the body.

If you really want to be a sensitive, intelligent mind, you need a sensitive, intelligent body too. Yes, the body has its own intelligence. Don't kill it, don't destroy it, otherwise you will be destroying your intelligence. But if it is respected, then it becomes something religious, spiritual, holy.

Anything that the society respects becomes a nourishment for your ego. And people are ready to do any stupid thing. The only joy is that it will bring respectability.

Self-cultivation is nothing but another name for ego cultivation. It is not a real path. In fact, no real path is needed. It looks like a long long, arduous path; it needs many lives. The people who have been preaching self-cultivation know perfectly well that one life is not enough; otherwise they will be exposed. So they imagine many many lives, a long, arduous journey of many lives. Then finally, after an unimaginable time, you arrive. In fact, you never arrive. You cannot arrive because you are already there. Hence this very idea of a path leading to a goal is meaningless.

Try to understand the paradox; it is very significant in understanding the spirit of Zen.

Zen is not a way, is not a path. Hence they call it the gateless gate, the pathless path, the effortless effort, the actionless action. They use these contradictory terms just to point toward a certain truth: that a path means there is a goal and the goal has to be in the future. You are here, the goal is there, and between you and the goal a path is needed, a bridge, to join you. The very idea of a path means you have yet to arrive home, that you are not at home already.

The second path—the pathless path, the path of enlightenment— has a totally different revelation to make, a totally different declaration of immense value: that you are already it. *"Ah, this!"* There is nowhere to go, no need to go. There is *no one* to go. We are already enlightened. Then only can it happen in an instant—because it is a question of awakening.

For example, if you have fallen asleep and you are dreaming . . . you can dream that you are on the moon. Do you think that if somebody wakes you up you will have to come back from the moon? Then it will take time. If you have already reached the moon, then you will have to come back and it will take time. The airship may not be available right now. There may be no tickets available; it may be full. But you can be awakened because it is only a dream that you are on the moon. In fact you are in your bed, in your home: you had not gone anywhere. Just a little shaking and you are suddenly back—back from your dreams.

The world is only a dream. We need not go anywhere; we have always been here; we ARE here and we are going to be here. But we can fall asleep and we can dream.

The All-Indian National Guard was out on maneuvers. They were about to begin a mock battle between the "red" team and the "blue" team when they received a telegram from Delhi: "Because of recent budget cuts we cannot supply weapons or ammunition, but please continue with your battle for training purposes."

The general called his troops together and said, "We will simulate the battle. If you are within a hundred yards of the enemy, point your arm and shout 'BANG-BANG' for a rifle. If you are within fifty feet, throw your arms over your head and shout 'BOOM' for a hand grenade. If you are within five feet, wave your arms and shout 'SLASH-SLASH' for a bayonet."

Private Abul was put on scout patrol, and apparently all the action went in another direction. He was out for three days and three nights, but did not see another person.

On the fourth day Abul was sitting under a tree, discouraged, when he saw a figure coming across the hill in his direction. He got down on his hands and knees and crawled through the mud and weeds, as he had been trained. Sure enough, it was a soldier from the other team.

Abul raised his arm and shouted "BANG-BANG!" but he got no response. So he ran up closer, threw his arm over his head, and shouted "BOOM!" very loudly. The other soldier did not even turn in his direction. So he ran right up to the soldier and shouted in his ear "SLASH-SLASH! SLASH-SLASH!" but still he got no reaction.

Abul was angry. He grabbed the other soldier by the arm and shouted, "Hey! You are not playing according to the rules. I went 'BANG-BANG,' I shouted 'BOOM,' and I came right up to you and said 'SLASH-SLASH,' and you have not even indicated that you have seen me yet."

At this point, the other soldier wheeled around to Abul and said in a deep voice, "RUMBLE-RUMBLE, I am a tank!"

This is the situation. You are not what you think you are, you are not what you believe you are. All your beliefs are dreams. Maybe you have been dreaming for so long that they appear almost like realities.

So the question is not of self-cultivation: the question is of enlightenment.

Zen believes in sudden enlightenment because Zen believes that you are already enlightened; just a certain situation is needed which can wake you up. Just a little alarm may do the work. If you are a little alert, just a little alarm and you are suddenly awake. And all the dream with all its long long desires, journeys, kingdoms, mountains, oceans . . . they have all disappeared in a single instant.

This beautiful story:

_____

The ancients said:
"(Self-)cultivation takes an unimaginable time. . . ."

_____

It is bound to take an unimaginable time because you will be fighting with shadows. You cannot conquer them, you cannot destroy them either. In fact, the more you fight with them, the more you believe in their existence. If you fight with your own shadow, do you think there is any possibility of your ever becoming victorious? It's impossible. And it is not because the shadow is stronger than you that the victory is impossible. Just the contrary: the shadow has *no* power, it has *no* existence, and you start fighting with something which is nonexistential—how can you win? You will be dissipating your energy. You will become tired and the shadow will remain unaffected. It will not get tired. You cannot kill it, you cannot burn it, you cannot even escape from it. The faster you run, the faster it comes behind you.

The only way to get rid of it is to *see* that it is not there at all. Seeing that a shadow is a shadow is liberation. Just seeing, no cultivation! And once the shadows disappear, your life has a luminosity of its own. Certainly there will arise great perfume, but it will not be something cultivated; it will not be something painted from the outside.

That's the difference between a saint and a sage. A saint follows the path of self-cultivation. He practices nonviolence, like Mahatma Gandhi; he practices truth, truthfulness; he practices sincerity, honesty. But these are all practices. And whenever you are practicing nonviolence, what are you doing? What is really happening inside you? You must be repressing violence. When you are practicing—when you *have* to practice—truth, what does it mean? It simply means untruth arises in you and you repress it and you go against it, and you say the truth. But the untruth has not disappeared from your being. You can push it downward into the very basement of your being; you can throw it into the deep darkness of the unconscious. You can become completely oblivious of it. You can forget that it exists, but it exists and it is bound to function from those deep, dark depths of your being in such a subtle way that you will never be aware that you are still in its grip—in fact, far more so than before because when it was consciously felt you were not so much in its grip. Now the enemy has become hidden.

That's my observation of Mahatma Gandhi. He observed, cultivated nonviolence; but I have looked deeply into his life and he is one of the most violent men this century has known. But his violence is very polished; his violence is so sophisticated that it looks almost like nonviolence. And his violence has such subtle ways that you cannot detect it easily. It comes from the back door; it is never at the front door. You will not find it in his drawing room; it is not there. It has started living somewhere in the servants' quarters at the back of the house where nobody ever goes, but it goes on pulling his strings from there.

For example, if ordinarily you are angry, you are angry with the person who has provoked it. Mahatma Gandhi would be angry with himself, not with the person. He would turn his anger upon himself; he would make it introverted. Now it is very difficult to detect it. He would go on a fast, he would become suicidal, he would start torturing himself. And in a subtle way he would torture the other by torturing himself.

In his ashram, if somebody was found drinking tea. . . . Now tea is so innocent, but it was a sin in Mahatma Gandhi's ashram. These ashrams exist by creating guilt in people; they don't miss any opportunity to create guilt. That is their trade secret, so no opportunity has to be missed. Even tea is enough; it has to be used. If somebody is found drinking tea, he is a sinner. He is committing a crime—far more than a crime, because a sin is something far deeper than a crime. If somebody was found . . .

And people used to drink tea. They would drink tea in hiding; they had to hide. Just to drink tea they had to be thieves, deceivers, hypocrites! That's what your so-called religions have done to millions of people. Rather than making them spiritual they have simply made them, reduced them to hypocrites.

They would pretend that they didn't drink tea, but once in a while they would be found red-handed. And Gandhi was searching, looking; he had agents planted to find out who was going against the rules. And whenever somebody was found he would be called . . . and Gandhi would go on a fast to punish himself.

"What kind of logic is this?" you will ask. It is a very simple logic. In India it has been followed for centuries. The trick is that Gandhi used to say, "I must not yet be a perfect Master, that's why a disciple can deceive me. So I must purify myself. You could deceive me because I am not yet perfect. If I was perfect nobody could deceive me. How can you imagine deceiving a perfect Master? So there is some imperfection in me."

Look at the humbleness! And he would torture himself; he would go on a fast. Now Gandhi is fasting because you have taken a cup of tea. How will *you* feel? His three days' fast for you, just for a single cup of tea! It will be too heavy on you. If he had hit you on the head it would not have been so heavy. If he had insulted you, punished you, told you to go on a fast for three days, it would have been far simpler—and far more compassionate. But the old man himself is fasting, torturing himself, and you are condemned by every eye in the ashram. Everybody is looking at you as a great sinner: "It is because of *you* that the Master is suffering. And just for a cup of tea? How low you have fallen!"

And the person would go and touch his feet and cry and weep, but Gandhi wouldn't listen. He had to purify himself.

This is all violence; I don't call it nonviolence. It is violence with a vengeance, but in such a subtle way that it is very difficult to detect. Even Gandhi may not have been aware at all of what he was doing—because he was not practicing awareness, he was practicing nonviolence.

You can go on practicing . . . then there are a thousand and one things to be practiced. And when will you be able to get out of all that is wrong in your life? It will take an unimaginable time. And then, too, do you think you will be out of it? It is not possible; you will not be out of it.

I have never seen anybody arriving at truth by self-cultivation. In fact, the people who go for self-cultivation are not very intelligent people because they have missed the most fundamental insight: that we are not going anywhere, that God is not something to be achieved; God is already the *case* in you. You are pregnant with God, you are made of the stuff called God. Nothing has to be achieved—only a certain awareness, a *self*-awareness.

There is an unusual store in New York where one can buy exotic foods from all over the world.

Mulla Nasruddin visited this store recently. He found rare tropical fruits from the jungles of South America and many strange delicacies from Africa and the Middle East.

In one corner he found a counter with several trays of human brains. There were politicians' brains at $1 per pound, engineers' brains at $2 per pound, and there was one tray of saints' brains at $50 per pound.

Since all the brains looked very much alike, he asked the man behind the counter, "Why do you charge so much more for the saints' brains?"

The man peered out from behind his glasses and answered, "Do you have any idea how many saints we have to go through to get a pound of brains?"

My observation of your so-called saints is exactly the same. I don't think they are very intelligent people—basically stupid, because unless one is stupid one cannot follow the path of self-cultivation. It *appears* only as a path; it is not. And it is tedious and it is long; in fact, it is unending.

You can change one habit; it will start asserting itself in something else. You can close one door and another door immediately opens. By the time you close that door a third door is bound to open—because basically you remain the same, the same old unconscious person. Trying to be humble you will simply become more and more egoistic and nothing else. Your humbleness will be simply a new way of fulfilling your ego. Deep down you will imagine yourself to be the humblest person in the world—there is nobody who is more humble than you. Now, this is ego speaking a new language, but the meaning is the same. The language is changed but the meaning is the same; translated into a different language it does not change. First you were the greatest man in the world, now you are the humblest man in the world, but you remain special, you remain extraordinary, you remain superior. First you were this, now you are that, but deep down nothing has changed. Nothing can ever change by self-cultivation.

A man spent thousands of dollars going from doctor to doctor trying to find a cure for his insomnia. Finally a doctor was able to help him.

"You must be terribly relieved," said one of his friends sympathetically.

"You said it!" replied the former insomniac. "Why, sometimes I lie awake all night thinking of how I used to suffer."

So what has changed? Self-cultivation only gives you a deception: the deception that something is happening, that you are doing something, that something great is on the way; that if not today, tomorrow it is going to happen.

Hornstein manufactured coats, but business was so bad the poor man could not sleep.

"Count sheep," advised Slodnick, his friend. "It is the best-known cure."

"What can I lose?" said Hornstein. "I will try tonight."

The next morning he looked more bleary-eyed than ever.

"What happened?" asked Slodnick.

"Sheep I could count," moaned Hornstein. "I counted up to fifty thousand. Then I sheared the sheep and made up fifty thousand overcoats. Then came the problem that kept me awake all the rest of the night: where could I get fifty thousand linings?"

No such things are going to help because if the *mind* is the same, it will go on creating the same problem in different ways. Basically the roots have to be transformed; just pruning the leaves is not going to help. And self-cultivation is only pruning of the leaves.

The ancients said:
"(Self-)cultivation takes an unimaginable time (while) enlightenment in an instant is attained."

Enlightenment is attained in a single moment. Why? Because you are already enlightened. You have simply forgotten it. You have to be reminded, that's all.

The function of the Master is to remind you, not to give you a path but to give you a remembrance; not to give you methods of cultivation, not to give you a character, virtue, but only awareness, intelligence, awakening.

In a single moment it can be attained because you have never lost it in the first place. You are dreaming that you are unenlightened. You can dream you are in heaven, you can dream you are in hell. And you know! You dream sometimes you are in heaven and sometimes in hell. In the morning you can be in heaven and by the evening you can be in hell. One moment you can be in heaven, another moment you can be in hell. It all depends on you. It is something to do with your psyche; it is not something outside you.

A man died, arrived at the Pearly Gates, and was shown by Saint Peter to a waiting room. He sat there, naturally anxious to know whether he would be sent to heaven or to hell. The door opened and a famous saint walked in.

The man rejoiced, "I must be in heaven!"

Just then the door opened again and a famous prostitute walked in. The man was confused. "In that case I must be in hell!" he thought.

While he was still wondering, the saint grabbed the prostitute and started making love to her. The man, flabbergasted, ran to Saint Peter and asked, "You MUST tell me: is this heaven or hell?"

"Can't you see?" answered Saint Peter. "It is heaven for him and hell for her!"

Heaven and hell are not geographical; they are not something outside you, they are something that belongs to your interiority. If you are awake, then you are in a totally different universe; it is as if in your awakening the whole existence becomes awakened. It takes a new color, a new flavor, a new fragrance. When you are asleep, the whole existence sleeps with you. It all depends on you.

So the question is not of cultivating any character, of becoming virtuous, of becoming a saint. The question is how to come out of dreams, how to come out of the past and the future, how to be just herenow.

That's what enlightenment is . . . *"Ah, this!"*

When Alice was at the Mad Hatter's tea party, she noticed that no jam was available. She asked for jam, and the Mad Hatter said, "Jam is served every other day."

Alice protested, "But there was no jam yesterday either!"

"That's right," said the Mad Hatter. "The rule is: always jam yesterday and jam tomorrow, never jam today . . . because today is not every other day!"

And that's how you are living: jam yesterday, jam tomorrow, never jam today. And that's where jam is! So you only imagine; you go on in a drugged, sleepy state. You have forgotten completely that this moment is the *only* real moment there is. And if you want to have any contact with reality, wake up herenow!

Hence this strange idea of Zen that enlightenment happens in an instant. Many people become puzzled: "How can it happen in an instant?" Indians particularly become very puzzled because they have the idea that first you have to get rid of all the past karmas, and now this foolish idea has reached the West. Now in the West people are talking about past karma: first you have to get rid of the past karma.

Do you know how long the past is? It is eternity! And if you are to get rid of all past karma you are never going to get rid of it—that much is certain. And meanwhile you will be creating other karmas, and the past will go on becoming bigger and bigger every day. If that is the only way out—that one has to get rid of all past karmas—then there is no possibility of enlightenment. Then there has never been any Buddha and there is never going to be any Buddha; it is impossible. Just think of all the past lives and all the karmas that you have built up—first you have to get rid of them. And how are you going to get rid of them? In trying to get rid of them you will have to create other karmas. And this is a vicious circle.

"And to be totally enlightened," the people who believe in the philosophy of karma say, "not only are you to get rid of the bad karmas, you have to get rid of the good karmas too—because bad karmas create iron chains and good karmas create golden chains. But chains are chains, and you have to get rid of all kinds of chains." Now things become even more complicated. And how can you get rid of bad karmas? If you ask them they say, "Create good karma to get rid of bad karmas." And how can you get rid of good karmas? Then the saints become angry. They say, "Stop! You are arguing too much. This is not a question of argument. Believe, trust, have faith!"

It is not really a question of getting rid of karmas. When in the morning you wake up, do you have to get rid of all the dreams first? You have been a thief in the dreams, a murderer, a rapist, or a saint . . . you can be all kinds of things in a dream. Do you have to get rid of all those dreams first? The *moment* you are awake you are out of all those dreams—they are finished! There is no question of getting rid of them.

That is the essential message of Zen: that you need not be worried about the past karmas; they were all dream acts. Just wake up and they are all finished.

But we are sleepy people and anything that fits with our sleep has great appeal. We listen only according to our state of mind. The whole world is asleep. There is rarely, once in a while, a person who is not asleep, who is awake. When he speaks to you there is misunderstanding, obviously. He speaks from his standpoint, from his awakening, and he says, "Forget all about your dreams—that is all nonsense! Good and bad, they are all alike; saint and sinner, they are all alike. Simply wake up! Don't be worried that first you have to become a saint in your dream, that you have to change your being a sinner into being a saint first, then you can wake up. Why go by such a long route? You can wake up directly! You can wake up while you are committing a sin; while you are murdering somebody in your dream you can wake up. There is no problem.

In fact, if you are a saint you may not like to wake up. A murderer will find it easier to wake up because he has nothing to lose, but the saint has great prestige to lose. Maybe he is being garlanded and a Nobel Prize is being given and people are clapping and touching his feet . . . and suddenly the alarm goes. Is this the time for the alarm? Can't the alarm wait a little more? When things are going so sweetly and beautifully the alarm can wait a little. A murderer has nothing to lose. He is already suffering; he is in a deep inner torture. In fact, he will feel relieved if the alarm goes off. He will feel a great freedom coming out of that nightmare.

Hence it happens more often that sinners wake up earlier than the saints, because the sinners go through nightmares and saints are having such sweet dreams. Who wants to wake up when you are a king with a golden palace and enjoying all kinds of things? Maybe you are in paradise in your dream.

But one thing is certain: when you are asleep you have a certain language—the language of sleep—and you can understand other people who are asleep and speak the same language. That's why the philosophy of karma became so important, so prevalent, so dominant. It has ruled almost all the religions of the world in different ways.

In India there have been three great religions: Hinduism, Jainism, Buddhism. They disagree on every point *except* on the philosophy of karma; they disagree on *every* point possible. They disagree on the existence of God, they disagree even on the existence of the soul, they disagree on the existence of the world, but they don't disagree on the philosophy of karma. It must have some deep appeal for the sleeping mind. And these people cannot understand Zen.

When a Hindu pundit or a Jaina monk comes to me he is very much puzzled. He says, "Are you teaching instant, sudden enlightenment? Then what about Mahavira who had to struggle for many many lives to become enlightened?"

I say to them, "Those stories are invented by you. The Mahavira that *you* talk about is an invention of your dream; you don't know about the real Mahavira. How can you know about his past lives? You don't even know about *your* past lives!" And there is not even any agreement on his last life among his followers—what to say about his past lives?

On such factual matters . . . for example, whether he was married or not: one sect of Jainas says he was not married, because to them a man like Mahavira getting married looks insulting, humiliating. And the other sect of the Jainas says he was not only married, but he had a daughter too. Now that is going too far—having a daughter! That means he must have indulged in sex—because at that time the story of Jesus had not happened. Virgin birth was not yet known!

They can't agree . . . the disciples can't agree about Mahavira's last life on factual matters like marriage, daughter, et cetera, and they talk about his past lives!

Anything that helps you to go on sleeping, postponing, appeals. "Even Mahavira had to work hard for many many lives, so how can *we* become enlightened in this life? It will take many lives, so there is no need to do anything right now. We can wait! And it is *not* going to happen right now anyway; it will take many many lives. Meanwhile, why not do other things? Accumulate more money, prestige, power. Do other things: eat, drink, be merry—because this is not going to happen, this enlightenment, right now; it will take many many lives. And meanwhile you cannot just go on sitting and waiting; one has to do something."

Sleeping people can understand a language which appeals to their sleep. We understand only that which triggers some process in our being.

The Sisters of Mercy were about to be sent as missionaries out into the world of sin. Mother Superior had one last question to ask each nun before deciding which of them were best fitted for the hazardous tasks ahead.

"Sister Agatha," she asked the first. "What would you do if you were walking along a deserted street at night and a strange man approached you and made indecent advances?"

"Oh, Holy Mother of God!" gasped the nun. "May all the saints forbid! Why, I would get down on my knees and pray to the Holy Virgin that my soul might be saved."

Mother Superior noted that Sister Agatha might be better suited to more domestic work.

The same question was asked of Sister Agnes, who replied, "Why, I would punch him in the nose . . . and then start running down the street as fast as I could, shouting 'Help, help!' "

Mother Superior noted Sister Agnes as one of the possible candidates for the missionary work.

Next she asked Sister Theresa, who began, "Well, first I would pull his trousers down . . ." Mother Superior choked a lit-

*tle, but Sister Theresa continued. "And then I would pull my
dress up, and then—"*

*"Sister Theresa," interrupted the senior nun. "Now what
kind of an answer is that?"*

*"Well," said the other, "I just figure that I can run faster with
my dress up than he can with his trousers down!"*

We understand only that which we *can* understand. The sleeping humanity can understand only certain things; it can *hear* only
certain things. The other things are not heard or even if heard they
are not understood; they are misunderstood.

Zen has been misunderstood very much. You will be surprised
to know that even Buddhists don't understand Zen.

Many orthodox Buddhists have come to me asking why I em-
phasize Zen so much, because it is not the main Buddhist tradition.
That is true; the main Buddhist tradition is against Zen. Zen seems
to be a little outlandish, a little eccentric, for the simple reason that
it brings such a totally new truth to you: *instant* enlightenment.
Never has any other religion emphasized it so much: that you are
capable of becoming enlightened right now—it is all up to you.

If the training is efficient, enlightenment will be attained in
   one fingersnap.

There is no path as such, but there is a certain discipline to
wake you up. That is called "training." Training has nothing to do
with your character but something to do with your consciousness.
Training simply means a certain space, a certain context has to be
created around you in which awakening is easier than falling

asleep—just like when you want somebody to be awake you throw cold water into his eyes. Not that you teach him to be virtuous, not that you teach him to be nonviolent—those things are not going to help him to be awake. But cold water, that is a totally different phenomenon; that is creating a context. Or you give him a cup of tea; that helps him to wake up. Or you tell him to jog, run, shout; that will help him to wake up more quickly.

All Zen methods are like that: cold water thrown in your eyes, a hammer hit on your head. Zen is totally different from other religions. It does not give you a certain character; it certainly gives you a context.

In days gone by, Ch'an Master Hui Chueh of Lang Yeh Mountain had a woman disciple who called on him for instruction. The master taught her to examine into the sentence: "Take no notice."

Now, this is creating a context. The Master told her to meditate on this small sentence: "Take no notice." And it has to be meditated on in different situations, in all possible situations. It has not to be forgotten any time; it has to be remembered continuously, whatsoever happens.

She followed his instruction strictly without backsliding.
One day her house caught fire, but she said: "Take no notice."

Now, this is creating a context. This is real training, this is discipline. The house is on fire and she remembers the instruction: "Take no notice." It is easy when the house is not on fire and everything is running smoothly, well, and you can sit silently in a small corner you have made in the house to meditate— then you can say, "Take no notice." It is easy, but it is not going to wake you up; it may even help you to fall asleep. But when the house is on fire it is difficult, very difficult. Your possessiveness is at stake, your life is in danger, your security is gone, your safety is gone. You may be just a beggar the next day on the street with nothing left.

But the woman must have been a real disciple.

She said: "Take no notice."

And not only did she say it, she took no notice. She relaxed, as if nothing was happening. And the moment you can see your house on fire and can see it as if nothing is happening, nothing happens. The house will be burned, but you will come out of that experience for the first time with clarity, with no dust on your mirror, with great insight. Everything is on fire! The whole life is on fire because we are dying every moment. Nothing is secure, nothing is safe. We only go on believing that everything is secure and safe. In this world of flux and change, where death is the ultimate end of everything, how can there be any security?

If you can see your own house on fire and go on meditating silently, relaxedly, in a deep let-go—take no notice—you will come out of it a totally different person, with a new consciousness, reborn.

Another day, her son fell into the water and when a bystander
called her, she said, "Take no notice."

Now even more difficult—because a house is, after all, a dead
thing. We can make another house, money can be earned again.
But your son falls into the water, is drowning . . . this is a more
difficult situation, more attachment—your own son. And for the
mother, the son is her extension, part of her, part of her soul, of
her being. Still she says, "Take no notice."

She observed exactly her master's instruction by laying down
all casual thoughts.

If this is possible . . . because these are the two problems in the
world: possessiveness of things and relationships with people.
These are *your* problems too. That's where people are asleep: either they are possessive with things or they are in heavy relationships with people. These are the two points which keep you clouded,
confused, unaware.

She passed both the tests. And if you can pass these two things:
if you can become aware that you possess nothing . . . use everything but possess nothing, and relate with people but don't become part of any relationship.

Relating is one thing, relationship quite another. Relating does
not take you into any bondage; relationship is a bondage. Love
people, but don't be jealous, don't be possessive. Relate with as

many people as possible, but remain free and let them also be free of you. Don't try to dominate and don't allow anybody to dominate you either.

Use things, but remember: you come into the world with empty hands and you will go from the world again with empty hands, so you cannot possess anything.

If these two insights become clear and you start taking no note, all casual thoughts will disappear from your mind. And all thoughts are casual, no thought is essential. The essential is silence; thoughts are all casual. When thoughts disappear, the essential surfaces. Great silence explodes in a tremendous melody. And that experience is liberating, that experience is divine.

One day, as her husband lit the fire to make fritters of twisted
 dough, she threw into the pan full of boiling (vegetable)
 oil a batter which made a noise.
Upon hearing the noise, she was instantly enlightened.

That's what I call . . . if you are ready, if the context is ready, then *anything* can trigger the process of enlightenment—*anything*. Just:

Upon hearing the noise, she was instantly enlightened.

Nothing special was happening, just an ordinary noise. You come across that kind of noise every day many times. But if the

right context is there, you are in a right space . . . and she was in
a right space: nonpossessive, unrelated to anything, to any person, nondominating. She was in a state of liberation, just on the
borderline. One step more and she would move into the world of
the Buddhas. And that small step can be caused by anything
whatsoever.

Upon hearing the noise . . .

That noise became the last alarm, the last straw on the back
of the camel.

. . . She was instantly enlightened. Then she threw the pan of
  oil on the ground, clapped her hands and laughed.

Why did she do that: "Clapped her hands and laughed"?
When one becomes enlightened, laughter is almost a natural by-
product; spontaneously it comes—for the simple reason that we
have been searching and searching for lives for something which
was already there inside. Our whole effort was ridiculous! Our
whole effort was absurd. One laughs at the great cosmic joke.
One laughs at the sense of humor that God must have or the existence: that we have it with us already and we are searching for
it. One laughs at one's own ridiculous efforts, long long journeys,
pilgrimages, for something which was never lost in the first place.
Hence the laughter, hence the clapping.

Thinking she was insane, her husband scolded her and said . . .

And of course, anybody who is still asleep seeing somebody suddenly becoming enlightened, clapping hands and laughing, is bound to think that the person has gone insane. This break through will look to the sleeping person like a breakdown; it is not a breakdown. But the sleeping person can't help it; he can understand only according to his values, criteria.

. . . He scolded her and said: "Why do you do this? Are you mad?"
She replied: "Take no notice."

She continues: her meditation is still there. She is following her Master's instruction to the very end. The husband is calling her mad and she says: "Take no notice."

The world *will* call you mad. The world has always been calling Buddhas mad. Take no notice. It is natural; it should be accepted as a matter of course.

Then she went to Master Hui Chueh and asked him to verify her achievement.

The master's functions are many. First: to help you to wake up, to provoke you into an awakening; to create the situation in which sleep becomes more and more difficult and awakening becomes more and more easy; and when for the first time you ARE awakened, to confirm it, because it is very difficult for the person himself. The territory is so unknown. The ego is lost, all old values are gone, the old mind is no more functioning. Everything is so new; nothing seems to be continuous with the old. There seems to be no way to judge, evaluate, be certain. One is in deep awe and wonder. One does not know what is happening, what has happened, what it is all about. One is simply at a loss.

Hence the last function of the Master is to confirm, to say, "Yes, this is it."

The master confirmed that she had obtained the holy fruit.

Zen people call this "the holy fruit," the fruition, the flowering—coming to the ultimate awakening, coming to the ultimate experience of yourself and existence. But remember: it can only happen in the moment. It can only happen in the instant. It can only happen now—now or never.

Remember this woman who was meditating on "take no notice." Such totality is needed. The house is on fire and she says: "Take no notice." Her son falls into the water and she says: "Take no notice." Her husband calls her mad and she says: "Take no notice." Then such a simple meditation—of taking no notice—creates the necessary milieu in which she becomes aflame, afire. Her inner being explodes. She is no more the same old person; she is reborn. She is reborn as enlightened. She becomes a Buddha.

You are all Buddhas—sleeping, dreaming, but you are Buddhas all the same. My function is not to *make* Buddhas out of you, because you are already that, but just to help you remember it, to remind you.

Enough for today.

Only the Gold

The brazen thief in the marketplace of Ch'i

Making the
choice
between
happiness
and
unhappiness

Once there was a man of Ch'i who wanted gold. At dawn he put
on his coat and cap and set out for the market.

He went to the stall of a dealer in gold, snatched his gold, and
made off.

The police caught him and questioned him. "Why did you snatch
somebody else's gold, and in front of so many people?"

The man replied:

"At the time when I took it I did not see the people—I only saw
the gold."[5]

---

[5] From *The Book of Lieh-Tzu: A Classic of the Tao*, by Angus Charles Graham. Copyright ©
1990 Columbia University Press. Reprinted with permission of publisher.

Let me tell you first one small anecdote:

> *"My doctor insisted that I come to see you," the patient told the psychiatrist. "Goodness knows why—I am happily married, secure in my job, lots of friends, no worries . . ."*
> *"Hmmm," said the psychiatrist, reaching for his notebook, "and how long have you been like this?"*

Happiness is unbelievable. It seems that man cannot be happy. If you talk about your depression, sadness, misery, everybody believes it. It seems natural. If you talk about your happiness nobody believes you—it seems unnatural.

Sigmund Freud, after forty years of research into the human mind, working with thousands of people, observing thousands of disturbed minds, came to the conclusion that happiness is a fiction: man cannot be happy. At the most, we can make things a little more comfortable, that's all. At the most we can make unhappiness a little less, that's all. But happy man cannot be.

Looks very pessimistic—but looking at the modern man it seems to be exactly the case, it seems to be a fact.

Buddha says that man can be happy, tremendously happy. Krishna sings songs of that ultimate bliss—*satchitanand.* Jesus talks about the Kingdom of God. But how can you believe so few people, who can be counted on the fingers, against the whole mass, millions and millions of people down the centuries, remaining unhappy, growing more and more into unhappiness, their whole life a story of misery and nothing else? And then comes death! How to believe these few people?

Either they are lying or they are deceived themselves. Either they are lying for some other purpose, or they are a little mad, deceived by their own illusions. They are living in a wish fulfillment. They wanted to be happy and they started believing that they were happy. It seems more like a belief, a desperate belief, rather than a fact. But how did it come to happen that very few people ever become happy?

If you forget man, if you don't pay much attention to man, then Buddha, Krishna, Christ, they will look more true. If you look at the trees, if you look at the birds, if you look at the stars, then everything is shimmering in tremendous happiness. Then bliss seems to be the very stuff the existence is made of. Only man is unhappy.

Something deep down has gone wrong.

Buddha is not deceived and he is not lying. And I say this to you, not on the authority of the tradition I say this to you on my own authority. Man can be happy, more happy than the birds, more happy than the trees, more happy than the stars—because man has something which no tree, no bird, no star, has. Man has consciousness!

But when you have consciousness then two alternatives are possible: either you can become unhappy or you can become happy. Then it is your own choice! Trees are simply happy because they cannot be unhappy. Their happiness is not their freedom— they have to be happy. They don't know how to be unhappy; there is no alternative.

These birds chirping in the trees, they are happy! Not because they have chosen to be happy—they are simply happy because they don't know any other way to be. Their happiness is unconscious. It is simply natural.

Man can be tremendously happy, and tremendously unhappy— and he is free to choose. This freedom is hazardous. This freedom is very dangerous—because you become responsible. And something has happened with this freedom, something has gone wrong. Man is somehow standing on his head.

You have come to me seeking meditation. Meditation is needed only because you have not chosen to be happy. If you have chosen to be happy there is no need for any meditation. Meditation is medicinal: if you are ill then the medicine is needed. Buddhas don't need meditation. Once you have started choosing happiness, once you have decided that you have to be happy, then no meditation is needed. Then meditation starts happening of its own accord.

Meditation is a function of being happy. Meditation follows a happy man like a shadow: wherever he goes, whatsoever he is doing, he is meditative. He is intensely concentrated.

The word "meditation" and the word "medicine" come from the same root—that is very significant. Meditation is also medicinal. You don't carry bottles of medicines and prescriptions with you if you are healthy. Of course, when you are not healthy you have to go to the doctor. Going to the doctor is not a very great thing to brag about. One should be happy so the doctor is not needed.

So many religions are there because so many people are unhappy. A happy person needs no religion; a happy person needs no temple, no church—because for a happy person the whole universe is a temple, the whole existence is a church. The happy person has nothing like religious activity because his whole life is religious.

Whatsoever you do with happiness is a prayer: your work becomes worship; your very breathing has an intense splendor to it, a grace. Not that you constantly repeat the name of God—only foolish people do that—because God has no name, and by repeating some assumed name you simply dull your own mind. By repeating His name you are not going to go anywhere. A happy man simply comes to see God is everywhere. You need happy eyes to see Him.

What has gone wrong?

I have heard about a man who became very famous in Germany—even today his statues are there and some squares and some streets are still named after him. His name was Dr. Daniel Gottlieb Schreber. He was the real founder of Fascism. He died in 1861, but he created the situation for Adolf Hitler to come—of course, unknowingly.

This man had very pronounced views on how to bring up children. He wrote many books. Those books were translated into many languages. Some of them ran into fifty editions. His books were loved tremendously, respected tremendously, because his views were not exceptional—his views were very common. He was saying things which everybody has believed down the centuries. He was the spokesman for the ordinary mind, the mediocre mind.

Hundreds of clubs and societies were set up to perpetuate his thoughts, his ideas, and when he died many statues were installed, many streets were named after him.

He believed in disciplining children from the time they were six months old—because he said if you don't discipline a child when he is six months old you will miss the real opportunity of disciplining him. When a child is very tender and soft, unaware of the ways of the world, make a deep imprint—then he will always follow that imprint. And he will not even be aware that he is being manipulated. He will think he is doing all this of his own will—because when a child is six months old he has no will yet; the will will come later on, and the discipline will come earlier than the will. So the will will always think: "This is my own idea."

This is corrupting a child. But all the religions of the world and all the demagogues and all the dictatorial people of the world, and all the so-called gurus and the priests, they all have believed in doing this.

This seems to be the basic cause why man is unhappy, because no man is moving freely, no man is sensing, groping his path with his own consciousness. He has been corrupted at the very root.

But Schreber called it discipline, as all parents call it. He believed in disciplining children from the time they were six months old in such a way that they would never after question their parents and yet believe that they were acting of their own free will. He wrote that on the first appearance of self-will one has to stop it immediately, kill it immediately. When you see the child becoming a person, an individual, you have to destroy the first ray of his individuality, immediately, not a single moment should be lost.

When the first appearance of self-will is noticed "... one has to step forward in a positive manner . . . stern words, threatening gestures, rapping against the bed . . . bodily admonishments, consistently repeated until the child calms down or falls asleep.[6]

"This treatment was needed only once or twice or at the most thrice," the doctor told people.

Make the child so afraid, shake him to his very roots! And those roots are very tender yet—a six-month-old child. Threaten him with gestures, with a deep hatred, enmity in your eyes, as if you are going to destroy the child himself. Make it clear to the child that either he can live or his self-will—both cannot be allowed to live. If he wants his self-will then he will have to die. Once the child comes to know that he can live only at the cost of self-will, he will drop his self-will and he will choose survival. That's natural! Survival one has to choose first; everything else comes secondary.

"And then one is master of the child forever. From now on, a glance, a word or a single threatening gesture is sufficient to rule the child."

What happened to his own children? Nobody cared. Everybody liked the idea. Parents all over the world became very enthusiastic and everybody started trying to discipline their children. And that's how, according to Schreber, the whole of Germany was disciplined. That paved the way for Adolf Hitler.

Such a beautiful country, intelligent, became the victim of a fool who was almost mad. And he ruled the whole country. How was it possible? It is still a question which has not been answered. How could he rule so many intelligent people so easily, with such foolish ideas?

These people were trained to believe; these people were trained not to be individuals. These people were trained always to remain in discipline. These people were trained that obedience is the

---

[6] Morton Schatzman, "Paranoia or Persecution: The Case of Schreber." *The History of Childhood Quarterly*, vol. 1 (Summer 1973), p. 74.

greatest virtue. It is not! Sometimes it is disobedience which is the greatest virtue. Sometimes, of course, it is obedience. But the choice has to be yours: you have consciously to choose whether to obey or not to obey. That means you have consciously to remain the master in every situation, whether you obey or you disobey.

What happened to his own children? Just now the whole history of his children has come to light.

One of his daughters was melancholic and her doctor suggested putting her in a mad asylum. One of his sons suffered a nervous breakdown and was institutionalized. He recovered, but eight years later had a relapse and died in a madhouse. His other son went mad and committed suicide. And the autopsies of both the sons proved that there was nothing wrong physically with their brains—still both went mad: one died in a madhouse, another committed suicide.

What happened? Physically their brains were perfect, but psychologically they were damaged. This mad father damaged all of his children. And that is what has happened to the whole of humanity.

Down the centuries, parents have been destroying people. They were destroyed by their parents, and so on and so forth. It seems to be a chronic state. Your parents were not happy; whatsoever they knew made them only more unhappy and more unhappy—and they trained you for it, and they have made a replica of themselves in you.

Arthur Koestler has coined a beautiful word for this whole nonsense. He calls it "bapucracy." "*Bapu*" means father—it is an Indian term. Indians used to call Mahatma Gandhi, "*bapu*." This word "bapucracy" is perfect. India suffers more than any other country from bapucracy. The Indian leadership is still suffering from its bapu, Mahatma Gandhi.

Each child is destroyed by the bapus. Of course, they were destroyed by their bapus. So I am not saying that it is their responsibility; it is an unconscious, chronic state that perpetuates itself.

So there is no need of complaining against your parents—that is not going to help. The day you understand it, you have to consciously drop it and come out of it.

Be an individual if you want to be happy. If you want to be happy, then start choosing on your own. There are many times when you will have to be disobedient—be! There are many times when you will have to be rebellious—be! There is no disrespect implied in it. Be respectful to your parents. But remember that your deepest responsibility is toward your own being.

Everybody is dragged and manipulated, so nobody knows what his destiny is. What you really always wanted to do you have forgotten. And how can you be happy? Somebody who could have been a poet is just a moneylender. Somebody who could have been a painter is a doctor. Somebody who could have been a doctor, a beautiful doctor, is a businessman. Everybody is displaced. Everybody is doing something that he never wanted to do—hence unhappiness.

Happiness happens when you fit with your life, when you fit so harmoniously that whatsoever you are doing is your joy. Then suddenly you will come to know: meditation follows you. If you love the work that you are doing, if you love the way you are living, then you are meditative. Then nothing distracts you. When things distract you, that simply shows that you are not really interested in those things.

The teacher goes on telling the small children: "Pay attention to me! Be attentive!" They are attentive, but they are attentive somewhere else. A cuckoo is crying with all its heart outside the school building, and the child is attentive—nobody can say he is not attentive, nobody can say he is not meditative, nobody can say he is not in deep concentration—he is. In fact, he has completely forgotten the teacher and the arithmetic that he is doing on the board. He is completely oblivious. He is completely possessed by the cuckoo. And the teacher says: "Be attentive! What are you doing? Don't be distracted!" In fact, the teacher is distracting.

The child is attentive—it is happening naturally. Listening to the cuckoo, he is happy. The teacher is distracting and the teacher says: "You are not attentive." He is simply stating a lie. The child was attentive. The cuckoo was more attractive to him, so what can he do? The teacher was not so attractive. The arithmetic has no appeal. But we are not born here to be mathematicians. There are a few children who will not be interested in the cuckoo. The cuckoo may go on getting madder and madder, and they will be attentive to the blackboard. Then arithmetic is for them. Then they have a meditation, a natural meditative state.

We have been distracted into unnatural motivations: money, prestige, power. Listening to the cuckoo is not going to give you money. Listening to the cuckoo is not going to give you power, prestige. Watching the butterfly is not going to help you economically, politically, socially. These things are not paying, but these things make you happy.

A real person takes the courage to move with things that make him happy. If he remains poor, he remains poor; he has no complaint about it, he has no grudge. He says: "I have chosen my way—I have chosen the cuckoos and the butterflies and the flowers. I cannot be rich, that's okay! But I am rich because I am happy."

This type of man will never need any method to concentrate, because there is no need—he is in concentration. His concentration is spread all over his life. Twenty-four hours he is in concentration.

Man has gone topsy-turvy. I was reading:

Old Ted had been sitting on the edge of the river for some hours without getting a bite. The combination of several bottles of beer and a hot sun caused him to nod off, and he was completely unprepared when a lively fish got himself hooked, tugged at his line and woke him up. He was caught completely off balance and, before he could recover, found himself in the river.

A small boy had been watching the proceedings with interest.

As the man struggled to get out of the water, he turned to his fa-
ther and asked, "Dad, is that man catching a fish or is that fish
catching a man?"

Man has gone completely topsy-turvy. The fish is catching you
and dragging you; you are not catching the fish. Wherever you see
money, you are no more yourself. Wherever you see power, prestige, you are no more yourself. Wherever you see respectability,
you are no more yourself. Immediately you forget everything—you
forget the intrinsic values of your life, your happiness, your joy,
your delight.

You always choose something of the outside, and you bargain
with something of the inside. You lose the within and you gain the
without. But what are you going to do? Even if you get the whole
world at your feet and you have lost yourself, even if you have conquered all the riches of the world and you have lost your own inner
treasure, what are you going to do with it? This is the misery.

If you can learn one thing with me, then that one thing is: be
alert, aware, about your own inner motives, about your own inner
destiny. Never lose sight of it, otherwise you will be unhappy. And
when you are unhappy, then people say: "Meditate and you will become happy!" They say: "Concentrate and you will become happy;
pray and you will become happy; go to the temple, be religious, be a
Christian or a Hindu and you will be happy!" This is all nonsense.

Be happy! and meditation will follow. Be happy, and religion
will follow. Happiness is a basic condition. People become religious only when they are unhappy—then their religion is pseudo.
Try to understand why you are unhappy.

Many people come to me and they say they are unhappy, and
they want me to give them some meditation. I say: first, the basic
thing is to understand why you are unhappy. And if you don't re-
move those basic causes of your unhappiness, I can give you a

meditation, but that is not going to help very much—because the basic causes remain there.

The man may have been a good, beautiful dancer, and he is sitting in an office, piling up files. There is no possibility for dance. The man may have enjoyed dancing under the stars, but he is simply going on accumulating a bank balance. And he says he is unhappy: "Give me some meditation." I can give him! But what is that meditation going to do? What is it supposed to do? He will remain the same man: accumulating money, competitive in the market. The meditation may help in this way: it may make him a little more relaxed to do this nonsense even better.

That's what TM is doing to many people in the West—and that is the appeal of transcendental meditation, because Maharishi Mahesh Yogi goes on saying, "It will make you more efficient in your work, it will make you more successful. If you are a salesman, you will become a more successful salesman. It will give you efficiency." And American people are almost crazy about efficiency. You can lose everything just for being efficient. Hence, the appeal.

Yes, it can help you. It can relax you a little—it is a tranquillizer. By constantly repeating a mantra, by continuously repeating a certain word, it changes your brain chemistry. It is a tranquillizer! A sound-tranquillizer. It helps you to lessen your stress so tomorrow in the marketplace you can be more efficient, more capable to compete—but it doesn't change you. It is not a transformation.

Just the other day, a small *sannyasin* asked me—whenever he comes he asks beautiful questions—very small, maybe seven years old. When he took *sannyas* . . . he must be courageous—he took *sannyas* before his mother decided to take *sannyas*; he took *sannyas* before his father decided to take *sannyas*. Has an individuality of his own. He took *sannyas* and I asked him, "Have you something to say?"

He said, "Yes, what group should I do?"

And the other night he came and I asked, "Now, what do you have to say?"

He said, "What do you think about Maharishi?" A seven year-old child!

I told him, "Maharishi is a good man, a very nice guy—but doing very ordinary work."

You can repeat a mantra, you can do a certain meditation; it can help you a little bit here and there—but it can help you to remain whatsoever you are. It is not a transformation.

Hence, my appeal is only for those who are really daring, daredevils who are ready to change their very pattern of life, who are ready to stake everything—because in fact you don't have anything to put at the stake: only your unhappiness, your misery. But people cling even to that.

I have heard:

In a certain remote training camp, a squad of rookies had just returned to their billet after a day's route-march under the boiling sun.

"What a life!" said one new soldier. "Miles from anywhere, a sergeant who thinks he's Attila the Hun, no women, no booze, no leave—and on top of all that, my boots are two sizes too small."

"You don't want to put up with that, chum," said his neighbor. "Why don't you put in for another pair?"

"Not likely," came the reply. "Taking 'em off is the only pleasure I've got!"

What else do you have to put at the stake? Just the misery. The only pleasure that you have got is talking about it. Look at people talking about their misery: how happy they become! They pay for it: they go to psychoanalysts to talk about their misery—they pay for it! Somebody listens attentively, they are very happy.

People go on talking about their misery again and again and again. They even exaggerate, they decorate, they make it look bigger. They make it look bigger than life-size. Why? Nothing do you have to put at the stake. But people cling to the known, to the familiar. The misery is all that they have known—that is their life. Nothing to lose, but so afraid to lose.

With me, happiness comes first, joy comes first. A celebrating attitude comes first. A life-affirming philosophy comes first. Enjoy! If you cannot enjoy your work, change. Don't wait! Because all the time that you are waiting you are waiting for Godot. Godot is never to come. One simply waits—and wastes one's life. For whom, for what, are you waiting?

If you see the point, that you are miserable in a certain pattern of life, then all the old traditions say: you are wrong. I would like to say: the pattern is wrong. Try to understand the difference of emphasis. You are not wrong! Just your pattern, the way you have learned to live, is wrong. The motivations that you have learned and accepted as yours are not yours—they don't fulfill your destiny. They go against your grain, they go against your element.

The village policeman stopped his son on the road as he saw him going home after a day's fishing.

"Any luck, son?" he asked.

"Yes, Dad," said the lad, opening his basket to show half a dozen lovely trout.

"That's marvelous! Where did you catch all those?"

"Just down there, Dad. There's a narrow lane marked PRIVATE *and you go down there until you come to a notice saying* TRESPASSERS WILL BE PROSECUTED. *A few yards farther on there's a pool with a big sign* NO FISHING ALLOWED—*and that's the place."*

Remember it: nobody else can decide for you. All their commandments, all their orders, all their moralities, are just to kill you. You have to decide for yourself. You have to take your life in your own hands. Otherwise, life goes on knocking at your door and you are never there—you are always somewhere else.

If you were going to be a dancer, life comes from that door because life thinks you must be a dancer by now. It knocks there but you are not there—you are a banker. And how is life expected to know that you would become a banker? God comes to you the way He wanted you to be; He knows only that address—but you are never found there, you are somewhere else, hiding behind somebody else's mask, in somebody else's garb, under somebody else's name.

How do you expect God to find you? He goes on searching for you. He knows your name, but you have forgotten that name. He knows your address, but you never lived at that address. You allowed the world to distract you.

It happened:

"I dreamt I was a kid last night," Joe was telling Al, "and I had a free pass to all the rides at Disneyland. Boy, what a time I had! I didn't have to choose which rides to go on—I rode them all."

"That's interesting," remarked his friend. "I had a vivid dream last night too. I dreamt a beautiful dreamgirl blonde knocked on my door and knocked me out with her desire. Then just as we were getting started, another visitor, a gorgeous well-stacked brunette, came in and wanted me too!"

"Wow," interrupted Joe. "Boy, would I have loved to be there! Why didn't you call me?"

"I did," responded Al. "And your mother told me you were at Disneyland."

God can find you only in one way, only in one way can He find you, and that is your inner flowering: as He wanted you to be. Unless you find your spontaneity, unless you find your element, you cannot be happy. And if you cannot be happy, you cannot be meditative.

Why did this idea arise in people's minds? That meditation brings happiness. In fact, wherever they found a happy person they always found a meditative mind—both things got associated.

Whenever they found the beautiful meditative milieu surrounding a man, they always found he was tremendously happy—vibrant with bliss, radiant. They became associated. They thought: happiness comes when you are meditative. It was just the other way round: meditation comes when you are happy.

But to be happy is difficult and to learn meditation is easy. To be happy means a drastic change in your way of life, an abrupt change—because there is no time to lose. A sudden change—a sudden clash of thunder—a discontinuity.

That's what I mean by *sannyas:* a discontinuity with the past. A sudden clash of thunder, and you die to the old and you start afresh, from ABC. You are born again. You again start your life as you would have done if there had been no enforced pattern by your parents, by your society, by the state; as you would have done, must have done, if there had been nobody to distract you. But you were distracted.

You have to drop all those patterns that have been forced on you, and you have to find your own inner flame.

Don't be too much concerned about money, because that is the greatest distraction against happiness. And the irony of ironies is that people think they will be happy when they have money. Money has nothing to do with happiness. If you are happy and you have money, you can use it for happiness. If you are unhappy and you have money, you will use that money for more unhappiness. Because money is simply a neutral force.

I am not against money, remember. Don't misinterpret me: I am not against money—I am not against anything. Money is a means. If you are happy and you have money, you will become more happy. If you are unhappy and you have money, you will become more unhappy because what will you do with your money? Your money will enhance your pattern, whatsoever it is. If you are miserable and you have power, what will you do with your power? You will poison yourself more with your power, you will become more miserable.

But people go on looking for money as if money is going to bring happiness. People go on looking for respectability as if respectability is going to give you happiness. People are ready, at any moment, to change their pattern, to change their ways, if more money is available somewhere else.

I have heard:

Mulla Nasruddin's daughter came home and she said she was pregnant and the richest man of the town was the father of the unborn child. Mulla Nasruddin was, of course, mad. He rushed with his gun toward the rich man's house; he forced the rich man into a corner and said, "Now you can breathe your last, or if you have any prayer to say to God, say it!"

The rich man smiled and he said, "Listen, before you do anything neurotic. Yes, I know your daughter is pregnant by me—but if a boy is born I have kept one lakh rupees in the bank for the boy. If a daughter is born I have kept fifty thousand rupees in the bank for the daughter."

Mulla took his gun away and said, "Sir, if something goes wrong, if there is a miscarriage or something, are you ready to give her another chance?"

Once the money is there, then suddenly you are no more yourself; you are ready to change.

This is the way of the worldly man. I don't call those people worldly who have money—I call those people worldly who change their motives for money. I don't call those people unworldly who have no money—they may be simply poor. I call those people unworldly who don't change their motives for money. Just being poor is not equivalent to being spiritual; and just being rich is not equivalent to being a materialist. The materialistic pattern of life is that where money predominates over everything. The nonmaterialistic life is that where money is just a means—happiness predominates, joy predominates; your own individuality predominates. You know who you are and where you are going, and you are not distracted. Then suddenly you will see your life has a meditative quality to it.

But somewhere on the way, everybody has missed. You were brought up by people who have not arrived. You were brought up by people who were unhealthy themselves. Feel sorry for them! I am not saying be against them; I am not condemning them—remember. Just feel compassion for them. The parents, the schoolteachers, the university professors, the so-called leaders of the society—they were unhappy people. They have created an unhappy pattern in you.

And you have not yet taken charge of your life. They were living under a misinterpretation—that was their misery. And you are also living under a misinterpretation.

It happened:

In the days of the British Raj in India, a young subaltern traveled to a distant part of the Punjab to join his first regiment. He reported to the colonel who welcomed him and then said, "You must understand, Skiffington-Smythe, that we need a very special type of officer out here. Someone who can handle the natives, someone who can think for himself and keep cool in a tight spot. So we have devised a little test which all new officers are requested to undergo. Are you willing to have a try?"

"Certainly, sir," said the keen young officer. "Anything you say, sir."

"Very good," said the Colonel. "Now, the test is quite simple. It's in two parts: first of all you must go down to the village marketplace, where you will take hold of the first woman you see, rip off her veil and kiss her full on the lips. This is quite a dangerous procedure, since the men here are very jealous of their womenfolk and carry wicked-looking knives with them at all times. So you must kiss this woman and make good your escape. Then you must go into the jungle and shoot the first tiger you see right

between the eyes. You must kill it with one shot—right between the eyes. All clear?"

"Yes, sir," replied the subaltern.

And with that the Colonel handed the young officer a rifle with one round, and one round only, up to the spout. The brave young man saluted, turned on his heel, and was gone.

A week later the Colonel heard a scratching at his door. He shouted for whoever it was to come in: the door slowly opened and a figure collapsed across the mat. It was Skiffington-Smythe!

Bruised, battered and bleeding from a dozen wounds, he crawled across the floor, hauled himself painfully to his feet at the Colonel's desk, saluted weakly and gasped, "Right, sir . . . where's this woman I've got to shoot between the eyes?!"

And when I look at you, I see the same problem. Something has gone very deeply wrong. You have misunderstood the instructions.

Meditation comes naturally to a happy person. Meditation comes automatically to a joyous person. Meditation is very simple to a person who can celebrate, who can delight in life. You are trying it from the other way—which is not possible. This is the whole meaning of this small Zen anecdote—simple and yet very significant.

Once there was a man of Ch'i who wanted gold. At dawn he put
   on his coat and cap and set out for the market.
He went to the stall of a dealer in gold, snatched his gold, and
   made off.
The police caught him and questioned him. "Why did you
   snatch somebody else's gold, and in front of so many
   people?"

The man replied:
"At the time when I took it I didn't see the people—I only saw
the gold."

It is a parable. It says: if you know exactly what you want, you
only see that. Concentration comes easy. If you know exactly what
you want, then the whole life and the whole world goes on its own
way—you don't see it even. You go like an arrow. You are not distracted.

But if you don't know what you are meant to be here, if you
don't know what your destiny is, if you don't know what you really
want, then everything is a distraction, then you are pulled in this
direction and that. Then continuously you go on being pulled in
many directions—and that creates a mess out of you.

You are pulled in so many directions at once that your personality becomes broken, split. Only fragments: one fragment going
to the north, another fragment going to the south. You are continuously in conflict. You don't know where you are going, because
you are not one any more. You become one when you know what
you want.

Many people come to me and I ask them: "What do you want really?" They shrug their shoulders. They say, "We don't know." Then
it is obvious that your life cannot have any organic unity in it. You
don't have any sense of direction. You have been misguided. But—it
is never too late. You can take possession of your life at any moment.
If you decide, then the first thing is: don't listen to the parental voice
within you, don't listen to the schoolteacher's voice within you.

You can do a small technique to get rid of all this. You can just
sit on your bed every night before you go to sleep, close your eyes,
and just try to feel: whatsoever you want, is it your own? Feel that
wanting, that desiring and try to find out, try to check it out, to
whom that voice belongs.

If you listen silently you will be surprised: your mother is say-ing, "Become a doctor!" And you will be able to know exactly who is saying this. Your father is saying, "Become rich!" Your brother is saying something else, your teachers are saying something else, your neighbors are saying something else.

And not only that: your father is saying something with his lips and another thing with his eyes; saying one thing, meaning an-other thing. He says, "Be honest, be true!" and you know he him-self is not honest and is not true. And you can see it in his eyes—children are very perceptive. They look deep; their eyes go very deep, they can penetrate—they can see the father is lying. He himself is not honest, he himself is not true.

It happens: he is inside the house and somebody knocks at the door, and he sends the child to tell him that the father has gone out. He lies! The father is saying, "Don't beat your small brother—you are stronger, you are bigger," and the father goes on beating him himself—and he is very strong and very big, and takes every advantage that he can. One thing he is saying, another thing the child is reading. He goes on reading the indirect message.

In the school something is taught, and life needs something else. Confusion arises, conflict arises, contradictions go on get-ting together, and then they pull you in different directions—then you are no longer together, your unity is lost. A child is born as an organic unity. By the time you have become young, you are no more an individual, you are no more a unity. You are a crowd, a mad crowd.

This you have to understand: it is something that you have learned from others. And remember—one of the basic truths of life—that which you have learned can be unlearned. That which you have learned from others is nothing natural to you: you can erase it. Just a conscious awareness is needed; it can be erased and the slate can become clean again.

So the first thing is to erase all that has been forced on you, and only then will you be able to listen to your own heart's voice.

Many people come to me and they say, "How to distinguish what is what—what is mind's voice and what is heart's voice?" It is difficult to distinguish right now: first you have to clean the mind. The heart's voice is very still and very small. The mind's is very noisy: it goes on shouting things. The heart whispers. The mind shouts.

Your father used to shout at you. Your mother used to shout at you. The teachers in the school used to shout at you. The mind shouts. God speaks in whispers. First this shouting has to be dropped, otherwise it is very difficult. And many people have followed Dr. Daniel Gottlieb Schreber's methods. They have put their voice in you at such an early stage that it seems as if it is your own heart's voice.

One thing is certain: you can never become anything other than yourself, and unless you become yourself you cannot be happy. Happiness happens only when a rosebush grows roseflowers; when it flowers, when it has its own individuality. You may be a rosebush and trying to flower as a lotus flower—that is creating insanity.

Erase the mind. And the way to erase it is not by fighting: the way to erase it is just to become aware.

Every night for at least one hour, sit in your bed and just watch from where you hear something—just go to the very roots of it. Trace it out, go backward, find out from where it comes. You will always find the source, and the moment you have found the source you will feel an unburdening. Suddenly it is no more yours—now you are not deceived by it.

It is slow work, but if you work, after a few months you will be feeling so clean—your book clean, nobody else writing in it. Then, only then will you be able to hear that still small voice. And once you hear it, the very hearing is like a sudden clash of thunder. Suddenly you are together, suddenly you have a direction—suddenly you know where your gold is. And then you don't see anybody; you simply go like an arrow toward your destiny.

It is very easy to follow your parents, it is very easy to follow your teachers, it is very easy to follow the society, it is very easy to be obedient—to be rebellious, to be on your own, is very difficult. But growth comes the hard way.

Let me tell you one small anecdote to end with:

There was once a farmer who, after a poor crop, complained: "If God would only let me control the weather, everything would be better, because He apparently does not know very much about farming."

That's true! Nobody has ever heard about God being a farmer—how can He know?

The Lord said to him: "For one year I will give you control of the weather; ask for whatever you wish and you will get it."

In the old days God used to do that. Then He got fed up.

The poor man became very happy and immediately said, "Now I want sun," and the sun came out. Later he said, "Let the rain fall," and it rained. For a whole year first the sun shone and then it rained. The seed grew and grew, it was a pleasure to watch it. "Now God can understand how to control the weather," he said proudly. The crop had never been so big, so green, such a luscious green.

Then it was time to harvest. The farmer took his sickle to cut the wheat, but his heart sank. The stalks were practically empty. The Lord came and asked him, "How is your crop?"

The man complained, "Poor, my Lord, very poor!"

"But didn't you control the weather? Didn't everything you wanted turn out all right?"

"Of course! And that is the reason I am perplexed—I got the rain and the sunshine I asked for, but there is no crop."

*Then the Lord said, "But have you never asked for wind,
storms, ice and snow, and everything that purifies the air and
makes the roots hard and resistant? You asked for rain and sunshine, but not for bad weather. That's the reason there is no
crop."*

Life is possible only through challenges. Life is possible only
when you have both good weather and bad weather, when you have
both pleasure and pain, when you have both winter and summer,
day and night. When you have both sadness and happiness, dis-
comfort and comfort. Life moves between these two polarities.

Moving between these two polarities you learn how to balance.
Between these two wings you learn how to fly to the farthest star.

If you choose comfort, convenience, you choose death. That's
how you have missed real happiness: you have chosen convenience instead. It is very convenient to follow the parental voice,
convenient to follow the priest, convenient to follow the church,
convenient to follow the society and the state. It is very easy to say
yes to all these authorities—but then you never grow. You are trying to get life's treasure too cheap. It requires that you pay for it.

Be an individual and pay for it. In fact, if you get something
without paying for it, don't accept it—that is insulting to you. Don't
accept it; that is below you. Say: "I will pay for it—only then will I
accept it." In fact, if something is given to you without your being
ready for it, without your being capable for it, without your being
receptive for it, you will not be able to possess it for long. You will
lose it somewhere or other. You will not be able to appreciate its
value.

Existence never gives you anything cheap—because given without any effort on your part, you will never be able to rejoice in it.

Choose the hard way. And to be an individual is the hardest
thing in the world, because nobody likes you to be an individual.
Everybody wants to kill your individuality and to make a sheep out
of you. Nobody wants you to be on your own. Hence, you go on

missing happiness, you go on missing direction, and, naturally, meditation has become impossible, concentration seems to be almost nonexistent. You cannot concentrate, you cannot meditate, you cannot be with anything for more than a split second. How can you be blissful?

Choose your own destiny. I cannot show it to you, what your destiny is—nobody else knows it, not even you. You have to sense it, and you have to move slowly.

First, drop all that is borrowed on your being and then you will be able to feel. It always leads you to the right place, to the right goal. The thing that you call conscience right now, it is not your conscience. It is a substitute—pseudoconscience, fake, counterfeit. Drop it! And by its very dropping, you will be able to see hidden behind it your real conscience which has been waiting for you. Once that conscience comes into your consciousness your life has a direction, meditation follows you like a shadow.

Yes, that man was right. He said:

———————————————————————

"At the time when I took it I did not see the people—I only saw the gold."

———————————————————————

When you have felt and sensed your destiny, you see only your destiny, you see only the gold.

Enough for today.

The Black-Nosed Buddha

*How a Zen nun's worship spoiled
her beautiful golden statue*

On the
consequences
of jealousy
and
possessiveness

A nun who was searching for enlightenment made a wooden
statue of Buddha and covered it with gold leaf. It was
very pretty and she carried it with her wherever she
went.

Years passed, and still carrying her Buddha, the nun
settled down in a small country temple where there
were many statues of Buddha each having its own
shrine.

The nun burned incense before her golden Buddha each
day, but not liking the idea of her perfume straying to the
other statues, she devised a funnel through which the smoke
would ascend to her statue only.

This blackened the nose of the golden statue and made it especially ugly.[7]

One of the greatest problems that is bound to face everybody who is traveling the path is to make a clear-cut distinction between love and attachment. They appear the same—they are not. They look alike—they are not. Rather, on the contrary, even hate is more similar to love than attachment. Attachment is just the contrary; it hides the reality of hatred and gives the appearance of love, it kills love. Nothing else can be so poisonous as attachment, as possessiveness. So try to understand this, then we can enter this beautiful story.

It has happened to many, it is happening to you—because mind is so confused between love and attachment. And those who look at things from the outside, they always become victims. Attachment is taken as if it is love, and once you have taken attachment, possessiveness, as love, you will always go on missing the real thing. You have chosen a false coin. Now you will not look for the real coin because you think this is the real. You have been deceived.

Possessiveness, attachment, is the false love. Hatred is better, because at least it is true, at least it is a fact. And hatred can become love any day, but possessiveness can never become love. You simply have to drop it to grow into love. Why does attachment appear like love? And what is the difference? The mechanism is subtle.

Love means that you are ready to merge yourself into the other. It is a death, the deepest death possible, the deepest abyss possible in which you can fall, and go on falling and falling. And there is

---

[7] From *Zen Flesh Zen Bones* (Compiled) by Paul Reps, Tuttle Publishing, a member of the Periplus Publishing Group. Reprinted with permission of publisher.

no end to it, there is no bottom to it, it is an eternal falling into the other. It never ends. To love means the other has become so significant that you can lose yourself. Love is surrender—unconditional; because if there is even a single condition then you are important, not the other; then you are the center, not the other. And if you are the center, the other is just a means. You are using the other, exploiting the other, finding satisfaction, gratification through the other—but you are the goal. And love says, make the end the other, and dissolve, and merge. It is a dying phenomenon, a death process. That's why people are afraid of love. You may talk about it, you may sing about it, but deep down you are afraid of love. You never enter into it.

All your poetries, all your songs about love, are just substitutes so that you can sing without entering into it, so that you can feel that you are loving without loving. And love is such a deep need that you cannot live without it; either the real or some substitute is needed. The substitute may be false, but at least for a time, for the time being, it gives you the feeling that you are in love. And even the false is enjoyed. Sooner or later you will realize that it is false; then you are not going to change the false love into real love—then you will change the lover or the beloved.

These are the two possibilities: when you come to know that this love is false you can change, you can drop this false love and become a real lover. The other possibility is to change the partner. And this is how your mind functions: whenever you feel, "This love has not given me the bliss it promised, rather on the contrary, I have become more miserable"—you think the other is deceiving, not that you are deceiving.

Nobody can deceive you except yourself . . . so you feel the other is deceiving, the other is responsible: change the wife, change the husband, change the master, change the god, move from Buddha's temple to Mahavira's temple, change your religion, change your prayer, don't go to the mosque, go to the church—change the other. Then again for a time you will have the feeling that you are in love, in prayer. But sooner or later again the false will be known—because it cannot satisfy. You can befool yourself, but how long can one befool oneself . . . ? Then again you have to change—the other.

If you come to realize the other is not the problem, that your love is false—you have been talking about it, you have not been doing anything to enter into it—you are afraid and scared. Love is deathlike, and if you are afraid of death you will also be afraid of love. In death only your body dies. The essential, the ego that looks essential to you, remains safe. The mind, which appears significant to you, is carried on further into another life. Your inner identity remains the same; only the outer garb, the clothes, change in death.

So death is never very deep, it is just superficial. And if you are afraid of death, how can you be ready to enter into love? Because in love not only the garb, not only the house, but you die—the mind, the ego dies. This fear of death becomes the fear of love, and the fear of love becomes the fear of prayer, meditation. These three things are similar: death, love, meditation. And the route is the same but you have to move on it. And if you have never loved you cannot pray, you cannot do meditation. And if you have never loved and meditated, you will miss the beautiful experience of death completely.

If you have loved, then death is such a beautiful and intense experience that you cannot compare it with anything in life. Life can never be so deep as death, because life is spread out over seventy, eighty years. Death is in a single moment—so intense; life can never be so intense. And death is the culmination, it is not the end. It is the culmination, the very peak; your whole life you have been making effort to reach it. And what stupidity—when you reach to the peak you are so afraid, you feel so dizzy, you close your eyes, you become so scared that you become unconscious. People die, they die in an unconscious state. They miss the experience.

So love can be helpful because love will prepare you for death, and love will prepare you for meditation also. In meditation you have to lose—the other is not there—you simply have to lose yourself. Love is deeper than death; meditation is even deeper than love, because the other is still there in love—you have something to cling to. And when you can cling, something of you survives.

But in meditation there is no other. That is why Buddha, Mahavira, and Lao Tzu, they deny the existence of God. Why? They know very well God is, but they deny the existence so that you have no support left for meditation. If the other is there, your meditation can become at the most love, devotion, but the total death is still not experienced. Total death is possible only when there is no other and you simply dissolve, you simply evaporate; there is nobody to cling to—then the greatest ecstasy happens.

The word "ecstasy" is very meaningful. This English word "ecstasy" is so beautiful and so significant; no other language has such a word. Ecstasy means to stand outside. Ecstasy means you are completely dead, and you are standing outside yourself and looking at this death, as if your whole existence has become a corpse. You are out of it and looking at your own death; then the supreme bliss happens. If I say it to you, you will be scared. If I say to you that you are in search of the supreme death, you will be scared—but you are in search of it. The whole of religion is the art of learning how to die.

Love means death, but attachment is not death. Love means the other has become so significant that you can dissolve yourself; you trust the other so much that you need not have your own mind—you can put it aside.

This is why people say love is mad, and people say love is blind; it is. Not that your eyes go blind, but when you put your ego aside, your mind aside, to everybody else you will look blind and mad. This is the state of madness. You are not thinking on your own. You trust the other so much that now there is no need to think, because thinking is needed if there is doubt. Doubt creates thinking, doubt is the base of thinking. If you cannot doubt, thinking stops.

If you cannot think, where is the ego, how can the ego stand? That is why ego always doubts things, never trusts.

If you trust, no ego appears—the ego is gone. Hence the insistence of all religions that only through faith and trust and love will you enter the temple of the divine—there is no other door to it. Through doubt you cannot enter, because through doubt you remain. In trust you are lost.

Love is a trust, a dissolving of the ego. The center moves to the other. The other becomes so significant—your very life, your very being. Not even a flicker of doubt comes to you. It is so peaceful, so beautiful, that not a flicker of doubt comes to you, not a ripple in the mind. Trust is complete, perfect. In that perfect trust there is a beatitude, a blessing. Even if you think about it you will have a small glimpse of it, what it can be. But if you feel it, it is tremendous, there is nothing like it.

But the ego creates a false trick. Instead of love it gives you attachment, possessiveness. Love says, be possessed by the other; ego says, possess the other. Love says, dissolve into the other; ego says, let the other yield to you, force the other to be yours, don't allow the other to move in freedom. Cut the other's freedom, let him become your periphery, your shadow.

Love gives life to the other; possessiveness, attachment, kills the other, takes the life of the other. That is why lovers, so-called lovers, always kill each other—they are poisonous. Look at a husband and a wife: once they were lovers—they thought they were lovers and then they started killing each other. Now they are two dead persons, they have become an imprisonment for each other. They are simply afraid and bored, scared of the other.

Once it happened: in a circus, there was a woman lion-tamer. And the fiercest lions were in her perfect control; she would order them and they would obey. And the greatest thing, when everybody's breathing would stop, was when the fiercest lion would

*be ordered to come near and he would come, and the lion-
tamer, the woman, would have a piece of sugar on her tongue,
and the lion would come and take the sugar from her mouth.
Everybody would go mad—so much excitement, everybody
would clap and show their appreciation.*

*One day Mulla Nasruddin was there. Everybody clapped but
he was not moved at all. He said, "Nothing, anybody can do
that."*

*The woman, the lion-tamer, looked scornfully at him and
said, "Can you do it?"*

He said, "Yes, anybody can do it—if the lion can do it."

Man is so afraid of woman—and this is through the experience
of love. Love, the so-called love, kills the other. Otherwise, why is
this world so ugly? So many lovers, everybody is a lover; the husband loving the wife, the wife loving the husband, the parents loving the children, the children loving the parents, and friends, and
everybody, relatives, the whole world is in love. . . . So much
love—and so much ugliness, so much misery?

Somewhere, something seems to have gone deeply wrong—in
the very roots. This is not love; otherwise, fear disappears—the
more you love, the less you fear. When love really comes to its totality there is no fear. But in possessiveness, fear goes on growing
more and more, because when you possess a person you are always
afraid he may leave you, he may go away—and the doubt is always
there. The husband is always doubting that the wife may love
somebody else. They become spies on each other, and they cut
each other's freedom so there is no possibility.

But when you cut freedom, when you cut the possibility of the
unknown, life becomes dead, stale. Everything becomes flat,
meaningless, a boredom, a monotone. And the more it happens,
the more you become possessive. When life is ebbing, when
the love is going, when something is going out of your hands,
you become more possessive, more clinging; you become more

protective, you create more walls and more prisons. This is the vicious circle.

The more prisons, the less life there will be. You will be more afraid that something is happening—and love is disappearing so create a bigger prison. Then love will disappear more, then a still bigger prison will be needed. And there are many subtle methods how to do it: jealousy, continuous jealousy, and possessiveness, to such an extent that the other remains no longer a person. The other becomes just a thing, a commodity, because a thing can be possessed easier than a person, because a thing cannot rebel, cannot disobey, cannot go away without your permission, cannot fall in love with somebody else.

When love becomes a frustration—and it will become a frustration, because it is not love—then you by and by start loving things. Look at people when they polish their cars, the way they look at their car—enchanted! Look at the romantic light that comes to their face when they look at their car; they are in love with their car.

In the West particularly, where love has been killed completely, people are in love with things or animals: dogs, cats, cars, houses. It is easier to love a thing or an animal; a dog is more faithful than a wife ever can be. You cannot find a more faithful animal than a dog—he remains faithful, there is no danger. A wife is dangerous. A husband is dangerous; any moment he can move away and you cannot do anything. And when he moves, your whole ego is shattered, you feel hurt. To protect from that hurt ever happening you start killing the husband or the wife, so they become just like cars and houses—dead things.

This is the misery though: that whenever you possess a person he becomes a thing—but you wanted to love a person, not a thing. Because a thing can be possessed, but a thing cannot be responsive. You may love a thing, but the thing cannot answer your love. You may hug your car, but the car cannot hug you. You may kiss your car, but the kiss cannot be returned.

*I have heard about Picasso: a woman, a fan of Picasso's, once
came to him and said, "I saw your self-portrait in an art gallery.
It is so beautiful, and I became so possessed by it, that I forgot
completely and kissed the portrait."*

*Picasso looked at the woman and said, "Did the portrait re-
turn the kiss?"*

*The woman said, "What are you asking? How can a portrait
return the kiss?"*

*And Picasso said, "Then that is not my portrait!" How can a
dead wife return the kiss? How can a dead husband return the
kiss?*

This is the misery: if you want to possess, you kill. And the moment you have succeeded the whole glory is lost, because now the
other cannot respond. The other can respond only in freedom, but
you cannot allow freedom because you are not in love. Love is
never possessive. It cannot be, by its very nature.

And not only loving a man or a woman: if you start loving a
Buddha you will repeat this whole thing. You will do the same, you
will be possessive there also. That is why so many temples have
been created—possessiveness. Christians think Christ belongs to
them. Christ cannot belong to anybody, but Christians think he
belongs to them; they are the possessors. Mohammedans think
Mohammed belongs to them. You cannot draw a picture of
Mohammed—you will be dragged to the court. You cannot make a
statue of Mohammed, because Mohammedans won't allow it. But
who are these Mohammedans? How did they become the possessors? They have turned Mohammed into a dead thing.

Nobody can possess Mohammed, nobody can possess Christ—
they are so big and your hands are so small. They cannot be possessed. Love can never be possessed; it is such a vital force, and
such an infinite force, and you are so tiny and so small, you cannot
possess it. But Christians have their Christ, Mohammedans have
their Mohammed, Hindus their Krishna, Buddhists their Buddha.

This has happened in religions so deeply, that religion, rather than becoming a blessing to the world, has proved dangerous. Through this possessiveness religion becomes the sect—then you go on worshipping this dead thing and then nothing happens in your life; and then you think something is wrong with religion. Nothing is wrong with religion. Mahavira could have transformed you. Krishna could have given you the light that he had, but you didn't allow him. Christ certainly could have become the salvation, but you didn't allow. Jews crucified him, and you—you have mummified him in the churches. Now he is a dead thing—good to worship, good to possess, but how can a dead Christ transform you?

And the priest knows it very well. That is why I have never come across a priest who is a believer. Priests are deep down always non-believers, because they know the whole business, and they know this Christ is dead. When they worship it is just a gesture, for show.

It happened once, it is an historic fact, that in the year 999, on December 31, there was a rumor all over the world, particularly in Christian communities, that the last day was coming on January 1; in the year 1000. On January 1, the last day of judgment was coming and the world was going to be dissolved and everybody was going to face the divine.

So, on December 31, 999, all the Christians all over the world closed their shops, closed their offices—people even distributed their things, because on the morning of January 1 there was going to be no world. People kissed and hugged each other, even went to their enemies to be forgiven, and there was a totally different world that evening. Everything closed, because tomorrow there was going to be no future. So why be an enemy? And why not love? Why not enjoy? People were celebrating—the last day was coming.

All over the world, Christians closed everything. Only the offices of the Vatican in Rome were open—because the pope knows well, the priests know well, that this is not going to happen, this is just a superstition. And they created the whole thing! But not a single thing was distributed from the pope.

Priests are in the know. They know that Christ is dead—and you are a fool, you are praying to a dead thing. But they cannot say that to you, because that is a trade secret; and only through it is exploitation possible. And it is in their favor, because if Christ is alive they cannot become the agents in between. An alive Christ will come directly to you; he will not allow a mediator, a broker. He will not allow it. Christ will not allow a priest to come and stand in between the lovers and himself—he will face them, he will come to you directly. So for priests, a live Christ is dangerous, only a dead Christ is good.

Priests never like a Mahavira when he is alive, they never like a Buddha when he is alive—they are always against when he is alive. When he is dead, they immediately come and organize around him, make a temple and start exploiting you. Priests are against a Mahavira, a Buddha, a Krishna, but they know that when they are dead their names can be exploited.

But you have to remember well that with your love, your prayer, your worship—if it becomes possessive—you are killing. And if you kill Krishna how can he transform you? How can he bring you to Krishna consciousness? Impossible!

Now we should enter this story. It is beautiful.

A nun who was searching for enlightenment made a wooden statue of Buddha and covered it with gold leaf. It was very pretty, and she carried it with her wherever she went.

Many things have to be understood—even word by word. A NUN . . . because this is the heart of the woman—to possess. That's why not a monk, but a nun. And don't think that only women possess; men also possess, but then they have the heart of

the woman, not of the man. Why is woman more possessive than
man? Because possession is out of fear. Man is less afraid than
woman, that's why—man is less afraid than woman. Because he is
less afraid, he is less possessive. The feminine mind is more
afraid, fear is natural to it, there is always a trembling. Because of
that fear woman is more possessive. Unless she is completely satisfied that she possesses, she is not happy. And when she possesses completely she cannot be happy, because the man is dead.
Only in freedom life exists.

Hence, in the story, a nun has been chosen. But remember well,
it doesn't make any difference if you are a man—your mind can still
be feminine. There are rarely men . . . You may be a woman and
still have a man's fearless mind. So the distinction is not through
sex, it is through attitudes. A man can be a woman, a woman can be
a man—the symbol is just to show the attitude. What attitude?

If you are a man and still possessive, you have a feminine
mind. If you are a woman and not possessive, you have a male
mind. It is said that Mahavira insisted that no woman can enter
into enlightenment unless she becomes a man. People took it literally, and they missed the point. They thought that no woman can
enter into enlightenment, so every woman who is striving will
have to be born in the next life as a man, and then only can she enter. This is foolishness—but no feminine mind can enter into enlightenment, that is true, because the feminine mind means fear
and possessiveness. And with fear and possessiveness, no love, no
meditation is possible.

One woman became enlightened. Jainas—the followers of Mahavira and followers of the tirthankaras—were much disturbed.
What to do? So they changed the name of the woman into the
name of a man, and they simply forgot the whole thing. A woman
named Mallibai became enlightened—what to do about the theory
now? So they changed the name, they call Mallibai, Mallinath. They
changed the statue, you will never find a woman's statue. And this
Mallibai—or Mallinath—she was such a rare being that they had to

concede tirthankarhood to her. So in twenty-four tirthankaras one is a woman, but you will never find her because the name given is Mallinath.

So one feels no woman has attained enlightenment. But it is true in a different, deeper sense; no feminine mind can enter— because fear cannot enter it, possessiveness cannot enter.

A nun who was searching for enlightenment made a wooden statue of Buddha . . .

And it is very difficult for a mind that is feminine—man or woman. But the mind, if it is feminine, will create a statue; you will create the other. You cannot be alone.

A statue means the "other" has been created. There is no one, but you cannot be satisfied with nothingness; something has to be there to cling to. Hence so many temples and so many statues— they are created out of the feminine mind. That's why you will not find many men in the temples whenever you go, but many women will be there. And if some men have come, those are the hen-pecked husbands. They have come with their wives, they have not come directly; they had to come just because of the wife.

When Mahavira preached, forty thousand people became his disciples—thirty thousand were women, only ten thousand men. What is the matter? And this is the ratio—this is the ratio with me also. If four persons come—three women, one man. And the man comes with difficulty and goes very easily, and the woman comes very easily and it is very difficult for her to go. She clings; it is very difficult for her to go.

But a feminine mind can create difficulties, barriers. If you start becoming possessive, then you miss. You have to remember: the fear has to be left—only then love arises. The fear has to be dropped, because the fear is of the ego. And if fear exists, the ego will persist; then you can create a statue and cling to the statue. This statue is not going to lead you to the ultimate, because this is your creation. You may cover it with gold leaf, it may look pretty, but it is a dead thing. You may make a golden statue, but it is not going to help—it is a dead thing.

It was very pretty, and she carried it with her wherever she went.

It became a burden, it had to be carried, protected. She couldn't sleep well because somebody might steal it. She could not go without it, because somebody else might want to possess it, it might be taken from her. Her whole mind became possessive around it. The statue became the center, the center of her possessiveness, fear, worship. But this is not love.

Years passed, and still carrying her Buddha, the nun settled down in a small country temple where there were many statues of Buddha each having its own shrine.

Years passed, nothing happened. Carrying a Buddha nothing can happen, because how can you carry a Buddha? You can only carry a statue. Buddha has to be lived, not carried. Buddha has to be loved, not possessed. You have to dissolve yourself in the Buddha, not carry him as your possession.

Buddha is alive if you dissolve into him. But then Buddha is dangerous, because you will never come back. It is a point from where no one can come back. Once you have fallen, you have fallen into it; there is no returning. There is fear and trembling, you are afraid you may be lost. And your fear is true—you are going to be lost.

But with a statue there is no fear, you can carry it. The statue can be lost someday, but you will not be lost. You can create another, even a prettier one, there is no difficulty—it is your creation. Go to the temples: what has man done? Created statues, his own creations. Now he is bowing down before them, weeping and crying, and the whole thing is false, because the base is false. Your tears, your prayers—to whom are you addressing them? Before whom are you weeping and crying? Your own creations, your own toys. Howsoever beautiful and costly, it makes no difference. But you are the creator of your gods, and before them you cry and weep and you think something is going to happen. You are simply acting stupidly. Temples are filled with stupid people. They are not aware of what they are doing, bowing down before their own creations. Now, how can this help you?

She carried . . . many years passed, many lives may have passed—and still carrying her Buddha she was nowhere. Just wandering from one place to another, from one life to another, from one mood to another, from one mind to another—but just wandering, reaching nowhere! Then she got fed up with the journey; the goal seemed nowhere to be achieved, the goal seemed nowhere to be coming closer.

So she . . . settled down in a small country temple where there were many statues of Buddha each having its own shrine.

But there were many statues of the Buddha. In China, in Japan, they have created very big temples for Buddha. In China there is one temple with ten thousand Buddhas, ten thousand shrines in one temple! Ten thousand statues! But even ten thousand statues are of no help. One Buddha is enough, ten thousand statues are not enough.

Why does the mind go on, working nonsense? One statue is not doing it, so create two. This is the arithmetic; two are not doing it, so create three—ten thousand statues! One man wandering among ten thousand statues and nothing is happening. Nothing is going to happen, because life never arises out of a dead thing, a man is never transformed out of a dead statue.

Seek a living Buddha. And if you cannot find a living Buddha, close your eyes and seek there. If you cannot find him without, you will find him within, because Buddhas are never dead. They are there, just to be sought—and they are always there. They may be just by the corner of your house, but you have never looked. Or you are so acquainted with the neighbor, with the corner, that you feel you know. Nobody knows—you may meet the Buddha in a beggar.

Just remain with open eyes. If you are carrying a statue, your eyes are closed. This woman may have missed many Buddhas because of this statue—because she thinks she already possesses. She already has the Buddha, so what need is there to look elsewhere? Then she settled in a temple—people who live with statues will always settle in a temple. People who live with statues cannot reach to the ultimate goal; they have to settle somewhere on the way, by the side of the way—a shrine, a temple.

Many people have settled in temples. They wandered and they searched and then they found that nothing can be found, it is impossible. Not because the goal is very far away—the goal is very near, nearer than you can conceive—but because they are carrying statues. Those statues have become their blindness; their eyes are closed with their statues, their hearts are burdened with their statues, words, scriptures—dead things.

I have heard:

*Once it happened in ancient days, a king, a very scholarly man,
wanted to marry a girl, but no ordinary girl would do. He
wanted a perfect woman, astrologically perfect. So he consulted
many astrologers. It was very difficult—many years passed, his
youth was almost gone. He was no longer young—because these
astrologers are difficult people, and mathematics takes time.
And then one woman would be found and one attribute would
still be lacking—not exactly perfect.*

Really, you cannot find anyone perfect. It is impossible, because perfection always means death. If someone is alive, it means
imperfect—that's why we say that whenever one is perfect, he is
born no more. Because how can you be born if you are perfect?
Then you have passed through this world, you have gained, grown,
you cannot be allowed back.

Then the king said to his advisers, "It is enough; if not perfect,
then approximately perfect will do. But my youth is passing, I am
almost thirty-eight. Now find a woman!"

So a woman was found—not exactly one hundred percent, but
ninety-nine percent. Then the search started for the right time
when this king should make love to this woman, because he
wanted a rare, extraordinary child. It was very, very difficult, many
scriptures were consulted, the *I Ching* and others; many wise men
were called from faraway countries, and they consulted and they
discussed—and the king was almost forty-four.

Then one day he got fed up, and he turned them out. He burned
all the scriptures and told to his wife, "Enough is enough! Now we
must make love"—they had not made love up to now. But the woman
was old, he was also old, and with love there is a problem. If you start
making love early, you can go on making love to the very end of your
life. If you don't start early, you cannot make love later on, because
lovemaking is a mechanical thing. The mechanism needs efficiency.

So if a man starts making love when he is fourteen, he may go
on making love up to eighty. And don't think that if you make
love too much in your young age, then in your old age you will
not be able. You are absolutely wrong. If you make love too
much, only then will you be able to later on. And you cannot
make love too much, remember that, because the body won't allow. Too much is impossible; there is a thermostat in the body—
too much is not possible. Whatsoever you do, it is always within
the limit. But by this time the king had become impotent—he
couldn't make love, the wife was frigid. They had missed the
right moment. The child was never born to them, then they had
to adopt a child.

This is what is happening: you have to adopt a Buddha, you
have to adopt a god. It is not born to you—and God must be born to
you, otherwise it is a false god. But you have been missing because
you are so occupied with scriptures, wise men, astrology, and all
sorts of nonsense. You are so obsessed with words, statues, temples, rituals, formalities, that by the time formalities are fulfilled
life has gone. By the time you conclude logically, life is no longer
there to do it.

This woman finally settled in a temple, and I tell you: never
settle in a temple, because a temple can only be a night's shelter, it
cannot be a permanent settlement. Never settle in a temple, never
settle in a sect, never settle with the Vatican, never settle with a
sectarian mind.

You can have a rest, that's okay. Stay there for a night, and by
the morning, before they catch hold of you, move! Go on moving—
unless you reach the ultimate; only that is the temple. But there
you will not find any statues. There you will find the real—not the
statue, not the portrait, but the real. Don't settle with a portrait,
don't settle with the false, don't settle with the carbon copy.
Search for the original, the very source.

The woman settled—she had to settle. When you carry a wooden
Buddha, how can you attain enlightenment? If wooden Buddhas can

give you enlightenment, then there will be no problem. A wooden Buddha is a wooden Buddha. You can carry it, you can play with it.

The nun burned incense before her golden Buddha each day.

The Buddha was wooden, just covered with gold, but she used to call her Buddha "Golden Buddha." The gold was just skin deep; deep down there was just a wooden Buddha, nothing else. But you can hide things, and through gold you can hide anything. When there is not love, then there is much gold around the wife. A wooden Buddha under the gold leaf—and you think everything is okay. And the wife also thinks everything is okay, because the husband every time comes and brings more and more ornaments. When love is dead, ornaments become very much alive. When there is love there is no need for ornaments.

You never cover a real Buddha with gold, do you? The Buddha won't allow you, he will simply escape. He will say, "Wait! What are you doing? You will kill me." Gold kills. Life can never be covered with gold—only death. Only death will allow you to do something. Life won't allow you such nonsense. But she called her wooden Buddha "Golden Buddha."

The nun burned incense before her golden Buddha each day, but not liking the idea of her perfume straying to the other statues, she devised a funnel through which the smoke would ascend to her statue only.

This is the mind of a possessive person: not even the per-fume, the incense, the smoke, is allowed to reach to other Buddhas—and others are also Buddhas. "But my Buddha is some-thing else. Your Buddha is nothing." In the temple all the other statues were Buddhas. It was not that somebody was a Krishna, or somebody was a Rama—then the difference would have been too much. She would not have stayed in that temple. But it was a Bud-dhist temple, so she could stay. But this was her statue, and those were not hers.

When there is really love, it doesn't bother to whom it reaches. When there is love, you love your beloved person, but you cannot devise a funnel so that your love reaches only to your beloved. Love is such a phenomenon that when it happens it goes on be-yond your beloved, always goes on and on and on. It spreads to everyone. It is just like a ripple on the lake.

If you throw a stone in the lake a ripple arises and then it goes on spreading and spreading to the very end. If you love a person, it is not linear, it is circular, a wave is created. When you love a per-son, you are throwing a stone in the lake of love. Now everybody will be benefited, not only the person you love. If you try to bene-fit only the person you love, you will simply do the thing this nun did. It is not possible. When there is someone who loves, his love goes on falling all around. You cannot channelize it, it is not such a thing—rivers can be channelized—it is oceanic, it cannot be chan-nelized. Attachment can be channelized, not love.

When you throw a stone in the lake, it falls at a particular spot, that's okay, but then the love goes on spreading. When you fall in love, you fall at a particular spot, with a particular person; but that is only the beginning, not the end. Then love goes on spreading, then the whole world is benefited. Whenever there is a single per-son of love, the whole world is benefited. There will be a center where the stone fell, from where the waves will arise and go on to the very end. There will be a center—the beloved, the lover; but the love cannot be contained there. It is a growing thing, nobody can contain it. So the lover becomes just the door, just the opening—and then the whole universe is benefited by it.

But this poor nun was just like you. Just a human mind, working through human stupidities. She did not like the idea of her perfume straying to the other statues—and the other statues are also of Buddha.

When I love a person, I find the divine there. Love reveals the divine in a person. Once it is revealed, all the statues of all the Buddhas. . . . Then everybody is divine; the tree is divine, the cloud is divine, the beggar on the street is divine, then everybody is divine. If love has happened and you have looked into the original face of a person—which is revealed only in love—then Buddhas everywhere are Buddhas, all the statues are Buddhas; then the whole world has become a temple.

But then you are not worried. Then you are not worried that your perfume is reaching somebody. You are not worried that your lover's perfume is reaching to somebody else. You will be happy that through you the whole world is being benefited, through you the whole world is receiving the blessing. If you are afraid and you try to contain it, then it is possessiveness and it will kill. Don't try to contain it, don't try to possess it. Allow it to grow, help it to grow, help it to reach to everyone. Only then you will receive it, because you can receive only when the whole world receives it.

But this is the problem: whenever you love a person, you want him to be contained, confined. It is as if you are confining a tree in a pot; not only the roots but the whole tree—then you will kill it. The tree has to move into the sky, it has to spread into the sky. Its flowers will give perfume to many, its branches will give shadow to many; many will be benefited by its fruits. Of course the roots are contained in you, but the tree goes on growing. And love is the greatest tree possible; it can spread into the whole sky, it cannot be confined, cannot be contained. You cannot make it finite—the very nature of love is infinite.

But not liking the idea of her perfume straying to the other statues, she devised a funnel through which the smoke would ascend to her statue only.

Then what happened? It was bound to happen:

This blackened the nose of the golden Buddha and made it especially ugly.

This is happening to every lover and beloved, because then the perfume is not perfume, it becomes just smoke; perfume needs to spread. Then the nose is blackened, and all the Buddhas now have black noses.

Look at your Krishna, look at your Buddha, your Mahavira; all their noses are blackened—because of you, your possessiveness. Your prayer is possessiveness, it is not real. Jainas won't allow anybody to enter their temples if they are not a Jaina. Hindus won't allow the untouchables, because they are not a higher caste. All the temples are blackened because they are possessed: "my temple." The moment I assert "my," it is no longer a temple, because how can a temple be mine or yours? A temple is simply a temple!

But all the churches, all the temples have become properties. They are mine or thine—then Buddha's nose is blackened, and it . . . *"made it especially ugly."*

All the temples, all the churches, have become ugly. They have to be really destroyed, cleaned, so the earth is clean. And the real temple can exist only then—when these temples disappear. They have become part of your market, of your legal system. They are now no longer symbols of the beyond.

Mind is such a thing; it turns everything into a possession, because the ego can exist only if it possesses. And ego is the barrier. Ego is the water in which only reflections can be caught, the real can never be known. Now drop this pail of water that can only reflect the moon! Why wait for an accident? Drop this old pail and let the water flow—no water, no moon.

Enough for today.

The Man Who Loved Seagulls

*. . . and why they stopped
playing with him*

A story
about the
futility
of chasing
happiness

There was a man living by the seashore who loved seagulls.
Every morning he went down to the sea to roam with the
seagulls. More birds came to him than could be counted in
hundreds.
His father said to him one day, "I hear the seagulls all come
roaming with you—bring me some to play with." Next day,
when he went to the sea, the seagulls danced above him
and would not come down."[8]

[8] From *The Book of Lieh-Tzu: A Classic of the Tao*, by Angus Charles Graham, copyright ©
1990 Columbia University Press. Reprinted with permission of publisher.

The greatest secret of life—and remember it always—is that life is a gift. You have not deserved it in the first place. It is not your right. It has been given to you, you have not earned it. Once you understand this, many things will become clear.

If life is a gift, then all that belongs to life is going to be a gift. Happiness, love, meditation—all that is beautiful is going to be a gift from the holy, from the whole. You cannot deserve it in any way and you cannot force existence to make you happy, or to make you loving, or to make you meditative. That very effort is of the ego. That very effort creates misery. That very effort goes against you. That very effort has destroyed you—it is suicidal.

In the American Constitution they have given a right, a basic right—and they call it the basic fundamental right—to pursue happiness. It is impossible to pursue happiness. Nobody has ever pursued it. One has to wait for it. And it is not a "right" at all. No court can force you to be happy or force happiness to be with you. No government violence is capable of making you happy. No outside power can make you happy.

The Founding Fathers committed a very deep mistake. It seems Thomas Jefferson didn't know much about happiness. Politicians can't know—they are the unhappiest people on earth. Jefferson added this right to the American Constitution, and you will be surprised that because of this, the very wording of it, America has become one of the unhappiest countries in the world, ever. Because the very idea that you can pursue happiness, that you can deserve it, that you can demand it, that you have the *right* to be happy, is foolish. Nobody has the right to be happy. You can be happy, but there is nothing like a right about it. And if you think that it is your right you will go on missing, because you have started to look in the wrong direction from the very beginning.

Why is it so? If life is a gift, all that belongs to and is intrinsic to life is going to be a gift. You can wait for it, you can be receptive to it, you can remain in a surrendered mood, waiting, patient, but you cannot demand, and you cannot force.

Emile Coué is more alert than Jefferson. Emile Coué has discovered a law he calls the Law of Reverse Effect. There are certain things which, if you try to do, you will undo. If you don't try to do them you may be able to do them. The very effort leads you to the reverse effect. For example, sleep. You want to go to sleep—what can you do? Everybody has a fundamental right to sleep, but what can you do? Can you ask the police to come and help? What can you do when you don't feel like going to sleep? Whatever you do is going to disturb you because the very effort works against sleep. Sleep is an effortlessness. When you simply relax, not doing anything, by and by you drift into sleep. You cannot *swim* toward it, you drift. You cannot make any conscious effort.

And this is the problem with all those people who suffer from sleeplessness, insomnia. All insomniacs have their rituals. They do certain things to cause sleep to come to them. And that is where they miss, that is where everything goes wrong. How can you force sleep? The more you force the more *you* will be there—aware, alert, conscious. Every effort will make you more aware, more alert, and sleep will be put off.

What do you do when you want to go to sleep? You don't do anything. You simply wait, in a restful mood. You simply allow sleep to come to you—you cannot force it. You cannot demand, you cannot say, "Come!" With closed eyes, in a dark room, on your pillow, you simply wait . . . and waiting, you start drifting. Like a cloud glides, drifts, you drift by and by from the conscious mind to the unconscious. You lose all control. You have to lose control; otherwise you cannot go to sleep, because the part that controls is the conscious mind. It has to allow. Control has to be abandoned completely. Then—you don't know when and why and how—sleep comes to you. Only in the morning you become aware that you have been asleep, and you slept well.

Ninety-nine percent of people who suffer from sleeplessness create their own trouble. I have not come across more than one percent of insomniacs who are really suffering from something in their body chemistry. Ninety-nine percent are simply suffering because they don't know Emile Coué's Law of Reverse Effect. They are followers of Jefferson; they think sleep is a "right."

In life, only on the surface, in the marketplace, do rights exist. As you move deeper, rights disappear. As you move deeper, gifts appear. This is one of the most basic things to remember always: you have not deserved life, and life is there! Absolutely unde-served, you are alive, with tremendous energy—alive! How does it happen? And if life can happen without deserving it, without any right to it, why not happiness? why not love? why not ecstasy? They can all happen, but you have to understand the law.

The law is: don't try directly. Happiness cannot be pursued. It can be persuaded. Persuasion is indirect. It is not an attack. You move, but not directly, because when you are direct you are ag-gressive. Nothing is as direct as violence, and nothing is as violent as directness.

Life moves in circles, not directly. The Earth moves around the sun. The sun moves around some greater sun. Galaxies move, the whole universe moves, in rounds. Seasons move in a round. Child-hood, youth, old age, move in a round. The whole of life is circular, it never goes directly. It is not like an arrow that goes directly to the target. The arrow is man's invention. In life there is nothing like an arrow. The arrow is man's violent mind. An arrow chooses the very shortest route between two points. The arrow is in a great hurry, seems to be too time-conscious. But existence is not in a hurry.

Just the other day I was reading a small booklet from "Jesus freaks"—ninety-nine percent nonsense, but one percent really beautiful! And even if something is one percent beautiful it is so much, because if you go to the Christian theologians, they are one hundred percent nonsense. The one percent that was meaningful, I loved. That part says, "Hurry kills! Haste is waste." And existence is not in a hurry, God moves with infinite patience. God is a loafer, he hangs around. In fact, God is not going anywhere—he is already there. So there is no goal. The arrow is dancing round and round and round; it is not going to any target—there is no target. Just *being* is the target. So God, existence, the whole, hangs around like the fragrance of a flower which hangs in a summer night—just around and around, nowhere to go.

And God has infinite patience. He works with care, and in very indirect ways. He creates a baby, and takes nine months—he doesn't seem to have any efficiency experts around him. This has been going on for millions of years, and he has not learned anything; otherwise he could have managed to create better instruments so that a baby could be created within nine minutes! Why nine months? And from the very beginning he has been doing the same thing; he has not learned anything. He should ask the experts, particularly the efficiency experts. They will show him how to produce, how to produce on a mass scale and not waste so much time—nine months per baby!

But it is not only with babies—with flowers also existence takes infinite care; with birds, even with a blade of grass, existence takes infinite care and time. It is not in a hurry. In fact it seems God is not aware of time at all. He exists timelessly. If you want to be with him, don't be in a hurry; otherwise you will bypass him. He will be always loitering here and now, and you will always be going there and then. You will always be like an arrow, and he is not like an arrow.

And to be with existence is to be happy, to be with existence is to be alive, to be with existence is to be in meditation.

But the whole training of man is how to do things fast. Speed in itself seems to be a value. It is not. In itself it can create only madness—and it *has* created madness.

Move indirectly. And what is indirectly?

I used to know an old man who was always complaining, always grumpy. Everything was wrong—he was a born critic. And of course as critics suffer, he suffered, because sometimes it was too hot, and sometimes it was too cold, and sometimes it rained too much, and sometimes it didn't rain at all. All seasons, all the year round, he was suffering. A negative mind, a negative attitude—and he was continuously in search of being happy, continuously making every effort to be contented and satisfied. But I have not seen a more discontented man than him; he was the very personification of suffering, dissatisfaction, discontent. In his eyes there was nothing but discontent. On his face many wrinkles of tension and discontent, all the grumblings of his whole life were written there.

But suddenly one day he changed. He had become sixty and the next day was his birthday. People came to greet him, and they could not believe their eyes—he had changed so suddenly, in the night. Somebody told me about it also, so I walked down to his house to inquire, because this was a revolution! The Russian revolution was nothing compared to it. The Chinese revolution, nothing compared to it. A revolution! For sixty years this man had trained himself for discontent. How, suddenly . . . ? What had happened, what miracle? I could not believe that even Jesus could have done such a miracle, it was not possible, because you never hear in the Bible. . . . Jesus cured blind men, he cured the deaf and dumb, he cured even the dead, but you don't hear a single story of Jesus curing anybody of discontent. It is not possible.

I asked the old man—he was really happy, bubbling with happiness—I said, "What has happened to you?"

He said, "Enough is enough! For sixty years I tried to be happy and could not, so last night I decided: now forget about it; don't bother about happiness, just live. And here I am, happy."

He *pursued* happiness for sixty years. If you pursue, you will become more and more unhappy. You are going direct, like an arrow, and God doesn't believe in shortcuts. You will attain to *your* target, but happiness will not be there.

Millions of people attain their targets. They wanted to be successful, they are successful—but unhappy. They wanted to be rich, they are rich—but unhappy. The richer they get, the unhappier they become, because now even the hope is lost. They were thinking that when they became rich they would be happy; now they are rich, and happiness . . . ? They cannot see any sign of it anywhere. Now, with unhappiness hopelessness also settles.

A poor man is never hopeless, a rich man always is. And if you find a rich man who is not yet hopeless it is certain he is not yet rich. Hopelessness is the symbol of being rich. A poor man can hope. Millions of things are there which he has not got. He can dream, he can hope that when these things are there he will have attained the target. Then everything will be okay, he will be happy.

This man pursued happiness for sixty years. At sixty death was coming nearer, and he must have felt it that night, because whenever a birthday comes a subtle feeling of death arises. To suppress that feeling we celebrate birthdays. Whenever a birthday comes, on that day it is impossible to forget death. To help you forget, friends come and greet you and they say, "This is your birthday." Every birthday is a death day, because one more year has gone, death is nearing. In fact a birthday is not a birthday, cannot be— death is approaching, death is coming nearer. Time is slipping fast through the fingers. The very earth on which you are standing is being pulled away. Soon you will be in the abyss. A birthday is a death day. To hide it, to suppress it, the society has created tricks. People will come with flowers and gifts to help you forget that death is coming nearer—and they call it a birthday.

He had become sixty. Next morning a new birthday was approaching. He must have felt, he must have heard the sounds, the footsteps, of death somewhere around . . . the shadow. And he decided: enough is enough. I pursued long—almost my whole life has been wasted in trying to be contented, and I could not be, so now I will do without. The old man said, "Now here I am. I have never been so contented as I am today, absolutely contented. There is no discontent, no unhappiness."

In the very search you create unhappiness. When you don't search, happiness searches for you. When you search, you search alone and you will not find. Where will you seek? How will you search? Mind can never be happy. Mind is your accumulated discontent. Mind is your accumulated unhappy past, the whole suffering that you have passed through: it is a wound in your being. And the mind tries to seek, to pursue, and you miss.

When you forget about happiness, suddenly you are happy. When you forget about contentment, suddenly it is there. It has always been there around you, but *you* were not there. You were thinking: somewhere in the future a target has to be achieved, happiness earned, contentment practiced. You were in the future and happiness was just around you like the fragrance of a flower.

Yes, God is a loafer. He is always loitering somewhere around. And you have gone too far, seeking. Come back home! And just be. Don't bother about happiness. Life is there as a gift; happiness is also going to be there as a gift—a gift from the whole, a holy gift.

When you are seeking too much you are closed; the very tension of seeking and searching closes you. When you are desiring too much, the very desire becomes such a tense state of affairs that happiness cannot penetrate you. Happiness penetrates you in the same way as sleep; contentment comes to you in the same way as sleep: when you are in a let-go, when you allow, when you simply wait, they come.

In fact, to say they come is not right: they are already there. In a let-go you can see them and feel them, because you are relaxed. In relaxation you become more sensitive—and happiness is the subtlest thing possible, the most subtle, the very cream of life, the essence. When you are relaxed in a total let-go, not doing anything, not going anywhere, not thinking of any goals, no target, not like an arrow but like a bow, relaxing, without tension—it is there.

I have heard a story about a great Mogul emperor, Babur, who conquered India. He became one of the greatest emperors in the

world, ruled almost the biggest part of the world any man has ever
ruled.

A man, a very wise man, came to see him, but the wise man was
very disappointed because Babur was talking to his court people
in such a profane way—vulgar, cracking jokes; ordinary, not refined even—and laughing a belly laugh. The wise man was disappointed. He said, "I was thinking that you were a cultured man,
and I have heard many stories that you love wisdom; that's why
I am here. I have heard that in your court you have many wise men,
learned men, scholars, musicians, philosophers, religious men,
and what do I see here? A simple vulgarity. It is intolerable. I cannot be here in your court a single moment more!"

Babur said, "Just one moment, then you can go. Look in that
corner." In that corner was a bow.

The wise man said, "What has that to do with the situation?"

Babur said, "I cannot be always tense. If the bow is always
tense, and the arrow is always on it, soon the bow will be broken. It
will lose its elasticity. It won't be flexible then, and a bow has to be
flexible; only then is it alive . . . the more flexible, the more alive.
That is my bow, and I am like my bow. Sometimes, yes, I am tense;
the arrow is on it, the bow is stretched. But only sometimes. Then
I rest and relax also."

I don't know what happened to that wise man. I feel Babur was
wiser than that wise man. A bow needs relaxation. You are also a
bow. You also need relaxation.

For small matters, the world of the market, you can move like
an arrow, because that is man-created. But for that which is not
man-created, you cannot be like an arrow—you have to be like a
relaxed bow.

God is total relaxation. Hence Patanjali says that perfect *samadhi*
is like sleep, with only one difference—otherwise the quality is the
same, the same flavor, the same taste—with just one difference: in
sleep you are unconscious, in *samadhi* you are conscious. But the

relaxation, the let-go, is the same. Everything untense, not going anywhere, not even a thought of going anywhere, just being here and now—suddenly everything starts happening.

You are not to do anything to be happy. In fact you have done too much to become unhappy. If you want to be unhappy, do too much. If you want to be happy, allow things, allow things to be. Rest, relax, and be in a let-go.

Let-go is the secret of life. Let-go is the secret of religiousness. Let-go is the greatest secret. When you are in a let-go many things, millions of things, start happening. They were already happening but you were never aware. You could not be aware; you were engaged somewhere else, you were occupied.

The birds go on singing. The trees go on flowering. The rivers go on flowing. The whole is continuously happening, and the whole is very psychedelic, very colorful, with infinite celebrations going on. But you are so engaged, so occupied, so closed, with not even a single window open, no cross-ventilation in you. No sunrays can penetrate you, no breeze can blow through you, you are so solid, so closed, what Leibnitz called "monads." You are monads. "Monad" means something without any windows, with no opening, with every possibility of opening closed. How can you be happy? So closed, how can you participate in the mysteries all around? How can you participate in the divine? You will have to come out. You will have to drop this enclosure, this imprisonment.

Where are you going? And you think that somewhere in the future there is some target to be achieved? Life is already here! Why wait for the future? Why postpone it for the future? Postponement is suicidal. Life is slow; that's why you cannot feel it. It is very slow, and you are insensitive; otherwise postponement is the only poison. You kill yourself by and by. You go on postponing—and you go on missing the life that is here and now.

For those who have attained to the here and now, the whole life starts showering flowers on them. Many things start happening that they never dreamed of.

When for the first time you are really relaxed in a meditative state, you cannot believe that life is so beautiful, so euphoric, such infinite bliss, you cannot believe it! It is unbelievable. When a Buddha reports, nobody believes. When a Jesus talks about his Kingdom of God, nobody believes. Even those who follow, they also are not absolutely trusting.

There is a story that Thomas was Jesus' most beloved disciple, but even he was not an absolute believer, even he doubted; hence the phrase "doubting Thomas." Thomas was the most beloved disciple, the closest—and yet he too was a doubting Thomas.

It happened that Jesus was moving from one shore of Lake Galilee to the other shore. He told his disciples to move ahead and he would be coming. So they moved off in a boat. Then suddenly, when they were just in the middle of the lake, they couldn't believe their eyes—Jesus was coming on the water, walking. They forgot everything about Jesus; they thought this must be a ghost. They had seen so many miracles, even the dead had been raised, but now they could not believe. They forgot everything in the moment of surprise, it was such an unbelievable phenomenon—Jesus walking on the water.

The disciples became so afraid and trembling, they started praying to God: "Save us! Who is this man coming? It must be a ghost! We are in danger." Even Thomas cried, "Who are you?" when Jesus came near.

Jesus said, "Can't you see me? Have you forgotten me completely? Can't you believe that I am Jesus, your master?" But still they were trembling.

Thomas said, "If you are really Jesus and not a ghost, or the Devil in disguise, if you are really Jesus, and if you are really walking on the water, then let me also walk on the water, master." This was a trick to test.

Jesus said, "Yes, you can come!" Then there was trouble. Thomas walked two, three steps. Yes, he could walk, but then the doubt arose: "Maybe this is the Devil playing a trick on me; otherwise how can I walk? It is impossible!" The thing was happening, he was walking on the water, but he couldn't believe it himself: a doubt arose and immediately he sank into the lake and Jesus had to run and bring him out.

And Jesus said, "You man of little faith." From that day the phrase "doubting Thomas" became prevalent. But he was the most beloved. The others were not even trusting enough to come out of the boat, even to *try*.

When Jesus brings the news, the good news of the Kingdom of God, nobody believes him. When Buddha talks about the infinite emptiness within, nobody believes him. We cannot believe! How can we believe unless we know? At least a glimpse is needed.

We live in such a suffering, hell, the news about the Kingdom of God seems to be just a dream, poetry maybe, but nothing more. Religion seems not more than literature, fictitious—great fiction, but nothing more. It has to be so, it is natural in a way, because you don't know where you are standing, what is happening all around you. You are so insensitive, closed. . . .

Open the windows, break the doors open! And run out of this imprisonment, stand under the skies. Feel again! Thinking won't help. Thinking can go on and on inside you without opening a single window. Only feeling brings you out of yourself—and you are so afraid of feeling, so much at ease with thinking and so afraid of feeling, because feeling will bring you out. It will bring you again into the very current of life. You will be in the river, moving toward the ocean.

Feel more, think less, and by and by you will see that the more you can feel, the more relaxed you are. The more you can feel, the more you become aware of the secret of life—that you need not do anything about it, you just have to be available. Just available, I say, and everything comes to you. Once the idea arises to catch hold, to cling, everything disappears. This is the meaning of this Sufi story.

There was a man living by the seashore who loved seagulls . . .

Love is the very center of all feelings, love is the soul of all feelings. All feelings hang on love. If you don't love, by and by all feelings will disappear. If you love, all feelings will be revived. And remember, I say *all* feelings: negative, positive, all. When you love, you start hating also—immediately. When you love, you start feeling anger also—immediately. When you love, you feel sad, you feel happy. When you love, all feelings are again back to life.

This is the trouble. That's why no society allows love; because if it were the case that with love only good feelings, feelings that society decides are good, came up, there would be no trouble. But with love, the trouble is that not only heaven starts flowering, but hell also. They are together, they are two aspects of the same coin. They cannot be separated—and there is no need to separate them, because a heaven without a hell would be poorer. A love without anger would be impotent. A love without sadness would be shallow.

Life is a polarity, and through polarities life becomes richer and richer and more and more complex. Life is not like ordinary Aristotelian logic, life is more like Hegelian dialectics: thesis, antithesis. Two polarities meet and fight, and a third phenomenon arises: synthesis. A greater harmony arises out of two polarities; then that greater harmony again becomes thesis, a new antithesis arises, then again a higher rung of the ladder of synthesis is reached.

This is how life moves. Life is Hegelian dialectics, it is not Aristotelian logic. It is not simple duality. It again and again reaches to oneness through duality—and that oneness again becomes a pole. It creates another pole; the movement starts. This is how life is trying to reach higher and higher pinnacles of being.

When you love you become happy, and you become sad also. These are the thesis and antithesis. Love is a harmony, the synthesis. Life moves through opposites, just like a river moves through two banks. You cannot conceive of a river with one bank. If you conceive of this, then all rivers disappear. If you try to ensure that one shore will be better, then rivers cannot exist.

That's what has happened to human consciousness. In the very beginning man decided against hate, against anger, against all negative poles, that they are not good. They are not good if they are alone, they are very bad. If a man is simply angry without love, he is mad. This anger is a disease. But if a man is angry because of love, a father angry with his child, with love, then anger has a beauty of its own.

No child will ever feel bad toward a parent who was angry with love. But a parent who was simply angry without love cannot be forgiven. The child may forget him, but he cannot forgive. Just anger, with no love? It is illness. It is poisonous. But if you are angry with love, the child understands. He understands your love, and in that bigger whole of love, the anger fits. It is just love in action, nothing else; and the child immediately feels it, and loves you more for it.

A husband angry without love is just ego, trying to possess, dominate. A husband angry with love is not ego trying to possess, but love trying to help. Even if anger is needed, love is ready to be angry.

When love arises, all feelings erupt; a volcano explodes and man becomes afraid. So it is better, man decided, not to touch this volcano. Let it be there, hidden, because it brings negatives also. But those who know, they say don't be afraid of the negative. The negative is bound to be there with the positive, like a shadow is bound to be with you. If you want no shadow, you will have to kill yourself. Then only can the shadow disappear. But nothing is wrong in a shadow. If you are there, nothing is wrong. If love is there, nothing is wrong.

Somebody asked Saint Augustine, "Tell me in one sentence, in a simple sentence, the whole message of Christ, because I am an ignorant man, and I cannot understand the subtleties of theology. And I don't know much about morality, so don't give me complex disciplines I may not be able to follow. Give me a simple discipline, so simple that I can understand and follow."

It is said Saint Augustine closed his eyes and meditated, and then he said, "Then there is only one thing—love, and everything else will follow."

Love is the greatest morality, because it brings the feeling part of you up, and the thinking part goes down. Nothing is wrong with the thinking part, but it is playing the role of the master, which is wrong. Reason is good if it helps feeling. Feeling should be the master and reason should be the servant. Feeling should guide and reason should manage. But if reason becomes the master and feeling has to follow, you will be dead . . . because how can you be alive only with reason? Life is feeling. Trees can exist without reason, but they cannot exist without feeling.

Now even scientists are becoming more and more aware that trees feel, and feel tremendously. Stars, rocks, rivers—they cannot exist without feeling. Feeling is their very life. Birds, animals, the whole—exist with feeling. Except man. Man is upside down. The head has become the prominent thing, and head has been suppressing feeling.

And it has happened all over life in that way. Politicians rule, dominate; in fact, poets should be the guides, not politicians. But as it happens in the atomic individual, so it happens on a vaster scale in society. If feeling rules the individual, then poets will rule life, then poets will rule nations. The world will be totally different. If the head rules, if reason rules the individual, then politicians will rule the world, and the world is going to be constantly in trouble, constantly at war, in constant conflict.

It is good to feel, and if feeling surrounds you, then there is nothing wrong in thinking. If thinking follows feeling—beautiful;

it helps. It is like a radar. It opens the way for the feeling to move on. It protects the feeling from dangers. It helps the feeling to know what is going to happen next, to plan a little. It is good! But good only as a servant.

If you love, you will have a deep affinity with existence. Trees will talk to you. Birds will start coming nearer to you. Animals will not be afraid of you—there is no need. Man creates fear because of his head. With his heart he is again one with the universe.

There was a man living by the seashore who loved seagulls. Every morning he went down to the sea to roam with the seagulls. More birds came to him than could be counted in hundreds. . . .

Thousands of seagulls gathered around him. They jumped and hopped, and they flew and they danced, and they moved with him on the shore. The man was accepted by the seagulls, because feeling is everywhere accepted. That is the language of existence: feeling. Reason is the language of humanity, not of existence—a local phenomenon, not universal. Feeling is the language, the forgotten language. If you understand feeling, you understand the whole.

It is said of Lukman, one of the wisest men ever born—he is the founder of Yunani medicine—it is said about Lukman that he would go to plants, to bushes, trees, sit there, feel them, and ask them, "What use can you be put to? What disease can you be helpful in?" And it is said that he discovered millions of herbs, just by feeling them. The herb would say, "It will be good if you use me in tuberculosis; I can help."

This looks like a myth, a fiction, but scientists have been at a loss: if this is a fiction, then how did Lukman come to know? . . .

Because whatsoever he knew has been proved by all scientific experiment to be right. And no laboratories existed then, like they exist today; not such refined instruments, not at all! If this is a fiction, then a greater problem arises: how did he come to know? And not one or two or a hundred herbs—millions! If he had been experimenting with crude implements then it would have taken at least ten to twenty thousand years for him to discover all that. That seems to be more fictitious. The first fiction seems to be nearer reality—that he asked.

And there is the same story in India also. Ayurveda, the Indian medicine, is based on the same secret. Those secrets were revealed by the plants themselves. But then a language is needed, a language which is universal and not local to humanity. Feeling is that language. Greek or Arabic or Sanskrit won't do. No language originating in the mind is divine language. No, the divine language originated in the heart. Feeling is the language.

If you start really feeling, and your heart starts really throbbing with feeling, you can ask a tree, and a tree is always ready to reveal its secret. You can ask a bird, and the bird is ready to reveal its secret. You can ask existence, and existence is ready to reveal its heart. That heart is God, the Kingdom of God, the ecstasy, the final liberation, *moksha*, nirvana; whatsoever you want to call it, you can call it.

More birds came to him than could be counted in
    hundreds . . .

He knew the language of feeling. It is love. Nobody is afraid of love, not even birds. And they can certainly feel more than you because they have no thinking apparatus, no disturbance of the mind.

In the West now they are experimenting with plants. They say that if you come near a plant with the idea to pluck the flowers, just with the idea—you have not plucked the flowers yet—if just with the idea you come near the plant then the whole plant starts trembling. A fear arises: the enemy is coming.

Now they have made very refined instruments which can check what emotion the plant is going through. If it is fear, then just like a cardiogram, on the paper the instrument records fear. If you come with the idea to water the plant, the whole plant feels happy. This is recorded, the instrument goes on recording that the plant is very happy. You water the plant, the plant is satiated, very thankful; in fact, showing all gratefulness toward you.

It happened in one of the laboratories in New York, suddenly it happened: a scientist was working on insects, and a plant was in the room, a cactus plant. He was working with earthworms, experimenting in many ways—and scientists, in the name of experiment, are torturing many types of insects, animals; he threw one earthworm in hot boiling water. He was also working with plants, and the cactus plant was accidentally connected with the instrument that records the feelings of the plant. Suddenly the plant went through much anger, fear, a very violent state. An earthworm had just been thrown into hot water!

Life is dying: a plant feels it. You cut one plant—the whole garden feels it, because everything is surrounded by an ocean of feeling, all around. You create vibrations. When you are angry you create vibrations. When you are lustful you create vibrations. When you are loving you create vibrations. Those vibrations are the universal language—they are understood by the whole existence.

It is said that when Buddha attained to enlightenment, trees flowered out of season. It may not be a fiction, it may be true. And one day we may be able to prove it scientifically, because if an earthworm, not related to a plant at all, of a totally different species, is thrown into hot water, and the death, the torture, the violence, is felt by the plant and the plant goes through a turmoil, a terrible turmoil, shaken to the very roots, then the other thing also seems possible.

Buddha attains to nirvana, he becomes enlightened. One life has reached the goal: it does not seem too fictitious that the trees around him suddenly flower out of season, in celebration. If pain can be felt, celebration can also be felt. Just a few steps more and science will be saying, "Yes, this is not a fiction." Life sometimes is stranger than fiction. It is.

His father said to him one day, "I hear the seagulls all come roaming with you—bring me some to play with" . . .

Now an idea had entered the head. The man was no longer the same. Love was not there. The heart was not functioning that day. A desire had entered, he had a target now. He had come to the seashore now with a business. He was no longer a friend to the seagulls—he was going to catch them—he was the enemy.

Next day, when he went down to the sea, the seagulls danced over him and would not come down.

The seagulls cannot understand what you are thinking in the mind but they can understand the vibes that you are creating around—and you are continuously creating vibes around you. You are a continuous broadcast of vibes, *continuous*. Whatsoever happens in your heart, it is just as if someone has thrown a stone in a lake: ripples arise, and they go on and on and on—they will go to the very end, to the very shore, all around. A feeling arises in you; immediately a stone has been thrown in the lake of your being. An idea arises in you—ripples arise. They go all around.

Those seagulls don't know exactly what the father has said to the son, because they don't understand the local language of man. They don't know what has really happened, but deep down they still know that this man is not the same. Somebody else has come, a stranger, not the old friend. Now he has come with an idea. The idea is not known, but throughout his whole body he is now not in a let-go. He has some idea to *do*, some plan, some desire. He is not the same relaxed man with whom seagulls could feel at home.

And this is the secret of the whole of life: not only seagulls but happiness, meditation, ecstasy—they all come to you when you are in a total let-go, in a deeply friendly mood, in a loving attitude to- ward existence. When you are at the heart, they come. When you are persuading them, and you think that happiness is something like a right, that you have to pursue it, suddenly the seagulls of happiness are not descending. They will dance above your head but they will never come down to play with you, to move with you, to jump and hop! No, they will never become one with you. They will not descend into your being.

Yes, happiness is a seagull. Meditation also is a seagull. Ecstasy is also a seagull. Existence understands only let-go. If you are in a let-go, you will attain. You will attain to whatsoever this existence can give you—and it can give you infinite blessings, infinite bene- diction. It can give you total satiety, contentment. You can become a buddha.

Existence is ready to give, but you are not ready to take it, be- cause you are thinking in terms of how to snatch it. Existence gives to you as gifts; you cannot snatch, you cannot conquer, you cannot achieve. You surrender, please. Please, be in a let-go.

All that is beautiful is like seagulls. Remember this: nothing can be done. The feast is already ready—you have been invited.

You can enter from the front door. But you are foolish, you are try-ing to enter from the back door, and in existence there is no back door. You are trying to enter like a thief. The front door is open for you, and the host is waiting on the steps to receive you, and you are trying to enter from the back door like a thief.

Life has no back doors. You cannot steal life. You cannot be a thief. Life gives, and gives infinitely and gives unconditionally. You please be just in a let-go. Let the seagulls descend and play with you, and loiter with you on the seashore. Everything is ready. The feast, the host—everything is ready, just waiting for you to come in from the front door. Effort is not needed. Effort is the back door. Effortlessness is needed.

Don't listen to Jefferson. Happiness is not a "right," you cannot pursue it. You have to persuade it. It is like a shy woman: you have to court it, indirectly. You don't go to a woman and say, "I would like to go to bed with you." That is too direct, too insulting, too vulgar. Any worthwhile woman would slap your face. One has to be a little more subtle with a woman. One has to be a little more indirect.

Patience is needed. Poetry is needed. And even if you have the idea in your mind to go to bed, that will be a disturbance, that will create an unbridgeable gap. If the idea is not there then you simply enjoy being with this woman. One day you will go to bed with her, but that will happen. The seagulls will descend on you.

Let life happen, don't try to force it. Through doing, only worthless things are achieved; through nondoing—all that is beau-tiful, all that is sacred, all that is divine.

Enough for today.

Looking for Treasure

How Rabbi Eisik got the
money for his shul

A story
about how
an impossible
dream came
true

Rabbi Bunam used to tell young men who came to him for the
first time the story of Rabbi Eisik, son of Rabbi Yekel of Cracow.

After many years of great poverty, which had never
shaken his faith in God, he dreamed someone bade him
look for a treasure in Prague, under the bridge which leads
to the king's palace. When the dream recurred a third time,
Rabbi Eisik prepared for the journey and set out for Prague.
But the bridge was guarded day and night and he did not
dare to start digging. Nevertheless he went to the bridge
every morning and kept walking around it until evening.

Finally, the captain of the guards, who had been watching
him, asked in a kindly way whether he was looking for
something or waiting for somebody.

Rabbi Eisik told him of the dream which had brought him here from a faraway country.

The captain laughed: "And so to please the dream, you poor fellow wore out your shoes to come here! As for having faith in dreams, if I had had it, I should have had to get going when a dream once told me to go to Cracow and dig for treasure under the stove in the room of a Jew—Eisik, son of Yekel, that was the name! Eisik, son of Yekel! I can just imagine what it would be like, how I should have to try every house over there, where one half of the Jews are named Eisik, and the other Yekel!" And he laughed again. Rabbi Eisik bowed, traveled home, dug up the treasure from under the stove, and built the house of prayer which is called "Reb Eisik's Shul."

"Take this story to heart," Rabbi Bunam used to add, "and make what it says your own: There is something you cannot find anywhere in the world, not even at the Zaddik's, and there is, nevertheless, a place where you can find it."[9]

Life is a search, a constant search, a desperate search, a hopeless search . . . a search for something one knows not what. There is a deep urge to seek but one knows not what one is seeking.

And there is a certain state of mind in which whatsoever you get is not going to give you any satisfaction. Frustration seems to be the destiny of humanity, because whatsoever you get becomes meaningless the very moment you have got it. You start searching again.

The search continues whether you get anything or not. It seems irrelevant what you have got, what you have not got—the search continues anyway. The poor are searching, the rich are searching,

[9] From *Tales of the Hasidim: The Early Masters/The Later Masters* by Martin Buber, translated by Olga Marx, copyright © 1947, 1948, copyright renewed 1975 by Schocken Books. Used by permission of Schocken Books, a division of Random House, Inc.

the ill are searching, the well are searching, the powerful are searching. the powerless are searching, the stupid are searching, the wise are searching—and nobody knows exactly what for.

This very search—what it is and why it is there—has to be understood. It seems that there is a gap in the human being, in the human mind; in the very structure of the human consciousness there seems to be a hole, a black hole. You go on throwing things into it, and they go on disappearing. Nothing seems to make it full, nothing seems to help toward fulfillment. It is a very feverish search. You seek it in this world, you seek it in the other world; sometimes you seek it in money, in power, in prestige, and sometimes you seek it in God, bliss, love, meditation, prayer—but the search continues. It seems that man is ill with search.

The search does not allow you to be here and now because the search always leads you somewhere else. The search is a projection, the search is a desire: that somewhere else is what is needed, that it exists but it exists somewhere else, not here where you are. It certainly exists, but not in this moment of time; not now, but somewhere else. It exists then, there, never herenow. It goes on nagging you; it goes on pulling you, pushing you, it goes on throwing you into more and more madness; it drives you crazy and it is never fulfilled.

I have heard about a very great Sufi mystic woman, Rabia al-Adawia.

One evening, people found her sitting on the road searching for something. She was an old woman, her eyes were weak, and it was difficult for her to see. So the neighbours came to help her.

They asked, "What are you searching for?"

Rabia said, "That question is irrelevant, I am searching. If you can help me, help."

They laughed and said, "Rabia, have you gone mad? You say our question is irrelevant, but if we don't know what you are searching for, how can we help?"

Rabia said, "Okay. Just to satisfy you, I am searching for my needle, I have lost my needle."

They started helping her—but immediately they became aware of the fact that the road was very big and a needle was a very tiny thing.

So they asked Rabia, "Please tell us where you lost it—the exact, precise place. Otherwise it is difficult. The road is big and we can go on searching and searching forever. Where did you lose it?"

Rabia said, "Again you ask an irrelevant question. How is it concerned with my search?"

They stopped. They said, "You have certainly gone crazy!"

Rabia said, "Okay. Just to satisfy you, I have lost it in my house."

They asked, "Then why are you searching here?"

And Rabia is reported to have said, "Because here there is light and there is no light inside."

The sun was setting and there was a little light still left on the road.

This parable is very significant. Have you ever asked yourself what you are searching for? Have you ever made it a point of deep meditation to know what you are searching for? No. Even if in some vague moments, dreaming moments, you have some inkling of what you are searching for, it is never precise, it is never exact. You have not yet defined it. If you try to define it, the more it becomes defined the more you will feel that there is no need to search for it. The search can continue only in a state of vagueness, in a state of dreaming; when things are not clear you simply go on searching, pulled by some inner urge, pushed by some inner urgency. One thing you do know: you need to search. This is an inner need. But you don't know what you are seeking.

And unless you know what you are seeking, how can you find it? It is vague—you think it is in money, power, prestige, respectability. But then you see people who are respectable, people who are powerful—they are also seeking. Then you see people who are tremendously rich—they are also seeking. To the very end of their life they are seeking. So richness is not going to help, power is not going to help. The search continues in spite of what you have.

The search must be for something else. These names, these labels—money, power, prestige—these are just to satisfy your mind. They are just to help you feel that you are searching for something. That something is still undefined, a very vague feeling.

The first thing for the real seeker, for the seeker who has become a little alert, aware, is to define the search; to formulate a clear-cut concept of it, what it is; to bring it out of the dreaming consciousness; to encounter it in deep alertness; to look into it directly; to face it. Immediately a transformation starts happening. If you start defining your search, you will start losing your interest in the search. The more defined it becomes, the less it is there. Once it is clearly known what it is, suddenly it disappears. It exists only when you are not attentive.

Let it be repeated: the search exists only when you are sleepy; the search exists only when you are not aware; the search exists only in your unawareness. The unawareness creates the search.

Yes, Rabia is right. Inside there is no light. And because there is no light and no consciousness inside, of course you go on searching outside—because outside it seems more clear.

Our senses are all extrovert. The eyes open outward, the hands move, spread outward, the legs move into the outside, the ears listen to the outside noises, sounds. Whatsoever is available to you is all opening toward the outside; all the five senses move in an extrovert way. You start searching there where you see, feel, touch—the light of the senses falls outside. And the seeker is inside.

This dichotomy has to be understood. The seeker is inside but because the light is outside, the seeker starts moving in an ambitious way, trying to find something outside which will be fulfilling.

It is never going to happen. It has never happened. It cannot happen in the nature of things—because, unless you have sought the seeker, all your search is meaningless. Unless you come to know who you are, all that you seek is futile, because you don't know the seeker. Without knowing the seeker how can you move in the right dimension, in the right direction? It is impossible. The first things should be considered first.

So these two things are very important: first, make it absolutely clear to yourself what your object is. Don't just go on stumbling in darkness. Focus your attention on the object—what you are really searching for. Because sometimes you want one thing and you go on searching for something else, so even if you succeed you will not be fulfilled. Have you seen people who have succeeded? Can you find bigger failures anywhere else? You have heard the proverb that nothing succeeds like success. It is absolutely wrong. I would like to tell you: nothing fails like success. The proverb must have been invented by stupid people. Nothing fails like success.

It is said about Alexander the Great that the day he became the world conqueror he closed the doors of his room and started weeping. I don't know whether it really happened or not, but if he was even a little intelligent it must have happened.

His generals were very disturbed. What has happened? They had never seen Alexander weeping. He was not that type of man, he was a great warrior. They had seen him in great difficulties, in situations where life was very much in danger, where death was very imminent, and they had not seen even a tear coming out of his eyes. They had never seen him in any desperate, hopeless moment. What has happened to him now—now when he has succeeded, when he is the world conqueror?

They knocked on the door, they went in and they asked, "What has happened to you? Why are you crying like a child?" He said, "Now that I have succeeded, I know it has been a failure. Now I know that I stand exactly in the same place as I used to be in when

I started this nonsense of conquering the world. And the point has become clear to mc now because there is no other world to conquer anymore—otherwise I could have remained on the journey, I could have started conquering another world. Now there is no other world to conquer, now there is nothing else to do, and suddenly I am thrown to myself."

A successful man is always thrown to himself in the end and then he suffers tortures of hell because he wasted his whole life. He searched and searched, he staked everything that he had, now he is successful—and his heart is empty and his soul is meaningless and there is no fragrance, there is no benediction.

So the first thing is to know exactly what you are seeking. I insist upon it because the more you focus your eyes on the object of your search, the more the object starts disappearing. When your eyes are absolutely fixed, suddenly there is nothing to seek; immediately your eyes start turning toward yourself. When there is no object for search, when all objects have disappeared, there is emptiness. In that emptiness is conversion, turning in. You suddenly start looking at yourself. Now there is nothing to seek, and a new desire arises to know this seeker.

If there is something to seek, you are a worldly man; if there is nothing to seek, and the question "Who is this seeker?" has become important to you, then you are a religious man. This is the way I define the worldly and the religious.

If you are still seeking something—maybe in the other life, on the other shore, in heaven, in paradise, in *moksha*, it makes no difference—you are still a worldly man. If all seeking has stopped and you have suddenly become aware that now there is only one thing to know—"Who is this seeker in me? What is this energy that wants to seek? Who am I?"—then there is a transformation. All values change suddenly. You start moving inward.

Then Rabia is no longer sitting on the road searching for a

needle that is lost somewhere in the darkness of one's own inner soul. Once you have started moving inward . . . In the beginning it is very dark—Rabia is right. It is very, very dark because for lives together you have never been inside—your eyes have been focused on the outside world.

Have you watched it? Observed? Sometimes when you come in from the road where it is very sunny and the sun is hot and there is bright light—when you suddenly come into the room or into the house it is very dark because the eyes are focused for the outside light, for much light. When there is much light, the eyes shrink. In darkness the eyes have to relax. A bigger aperture is needed in darkness; in light a smaller aperture is enough. That's how the camera functions and that's how your eye functions. The camera has been invented along the lines of the human eye. So when you suddenly come from the outside, your own house looks dark. But if you sit a little while, by and by the darkness disappears. There is more light; your eyes are settling.

For many lives together you have been outside in the hot sun, in the world, so when you go in you have completely forgotten how to enter and how to readjust your eyes. Meditation is nothing but a readjustment of your vision, a readjustment of your seeing faculty, of your eyes. In India that is what is called your third eye. It is not an eye somewhere, it is a readjustment, a total readjustment of your vision. By and by the darkness is no longer dark; a subtle, suffused light starts being felt.

And if you go on looking inside—it takes time—gradually, slowly, you start feeling a beautiful light inside. But it is not aggressive light; it is not like the sun, it is more like the moon. It is not glaring, it is not dazzling, it is very cool; it is not hot, it is very compassionate, it is very soothing, it is a balm.

By and by, when you have got adjusted to the inside light, you will see that you are the very source. The seeker is the sought. Then you will see that the treasure is within you and the whole problem was that you were seeking for it outside. You were seeking for it somewhere outside and it has always been there inside you, it has always been here within you. You were seeking in a wrong direction, that's all.

Everything is available to you as much as it is available to anyone else, as much as it is available to a Buddha, to a Baal-Shem, to a Moses, to Mohammed. It is all available to you, only you are looking in the wrong direction. As far as the treasure is concerned you are not poorer than Buddha or Mohammed—no, God has never created a poor man. It does not happen, it cannot happen—because God creates you out of his richness. How can he create a poor man? You are his overflowing, you are part of his being, how can you be poor? You are rich, infinitely rich, as rich as God himself.

But you are looking in the wrong direction. The direction is wrong, that's why you go on missing. And it is not that you will not succeed in life, you can succeed, but still you will be a failure. Nothing is going to satisfy you because nothing can be attained in the outside world which can be comparable to the inner treasure, to the inner light, to the inner bliss.

Now this story. This story is tremendously meaningful.

Rabbi Bunam used to tell young men who came to him for the first time the story of Rabbi Eisik, son of Rabbi Yekel of Cracow.

After many years of great poverty, which had never shaken his faith in God, he dreamed someone bade him look for a treasure in Prague, under the bridge which leads to the king's palace. When the dream recurred a third time, Rabbi Eisik prepared for the journey and set out for Prague. But the bridge was guarded day and night and he did not dare to start digging. Nevertheless he went to the bridge every morning and kept walking around it until evening.

Finally, the captain of the guards, who had been watching him, asked in a kindly way whether he was looking for something or waiting for somebody.

Rabbi Eisik told him of the dream which had brought him here from a faraway country.

The captain laughed: "And so to please the dream, you poor fellow wore out your shoes to come here! As for having faith in dreams, if I had had it, I should have had to get going when a dream once told me to go to Cracow and dig for treasure under the stove in the room of a Jew—Eisik, son of Yekel, that was the name! Eisik, son of Yekel! I can just imagine what it would be like, how I should have to try every house over there, where one half of the Jews are named Eisik, and the other Yekel!" And he laughed again. Rabbi Eisik bowed, traveled home, dug up the treasure from under the stove, and built the house of prayer which is called "Reb Eisik's Shul."

"Take this story to heart," Rabbi Bunam used to add, "and make what it says your own: There is something you cannot find anywhere in the world, not even at the Zaddik's, and there is, nevertheless, a place where you can find it."

The first thing to be understood about the story is that he dreamed. All desiring is dreaming and all dreaming takes you away from you—that is the very nature of the dream.

You may be sleeping in Poona and you may dream of Philadelphia. In the morning you will not wake up in Philadelphia, you will wake up in Poona. In a dream you can be anywhere; a dream has a tremendous freedom because it is unreal. In a dream you can be anywhere: on the moon, on Mars. You can choose any planet, it is your game. In a dream you can be anywhere, there is only one place you cannot be—that is where you are. This is the first thing to be understood about the dreaming consciousness. If you are where you are, then the dream cannot exist, because then there is no point in the dream, then there is no meaning in the dream. If you are exactly where you are and you are exactly what you are, then how can the dream exist? The dream can exist only if you go away from you. You may be a poor man and you dream about being an emperor. You may be an ordinary man and you dream about yourself being extraordinary. You walk on the earth and you dream that you fly in the sky. The dream has to be a falsification of reality; the dream has to be something else than reality.

In reality there is no dreaming, so those who want to know the real have to stop dreaming. In India we have divided human consciousness into four stages. We call the first stage the ordinary waking consciousness. Right now you are in the ordinary waking consciousness. What is an ordinary waking consciousness? You appear to be awake but you are not. You are a little bit awake, but that little bit is so small that it doesn't make much difference.

You can walk to your home, you can recognize your wife or your husband, you can drive your car . . . that little bit is only enough for this. It gives you a sort of efficiency—that's all. But it is a very small consciousness, exhausted very easily, lost very easily. If somebody insults you it is lost, it is exhausted. If somebody insults you, you become angry. You are no longer conscious. That's why after anger many people say, "Why did I do it? How did I do it? How could I do it? It happened in spite of me." Yes, they are right— it happened in spite of you because you lost your consciousness. In anger, in violent rage, people are possessed; they do things they would never do if they were a little aware. They can kill, they can destroy; they can even destroy themselves.

The ordinary waking consciousness is only "waking" for name's sake—deep down dreams continue. Just a small tip of the iceberg is alert—most of the thing is underneath, in darkness. Watch it sometimes. Just anywhere close your eyes and look within: you will see dreams floating like clouds surrounding you. You can sit on the chair any moment of the day, close your eyes, relax, and suddenly you see that the dreams have started. In fact they have not started, they were continuing—just as during the day stars disappear from the sky. They don't really disappear, they are there, but because of the light of the sun you don't see them. If you go into a deep well, a very deep, dark well, from the dark well you can look at the sky and you will be able to recognize a few stars—even at midday. The stars are there; when night comes they don't reappear, they have always been there, all twenty-four hours. They don't go anywhere, the sunlight just hides them.

Exactly the same is the case with your dreaming: it is just below the surface, just underground it continues. On the top of it is a little layer of awareness, underneath are a thousand and one dreams. Close your eyes any time and you will find yourself dreaming.

That's why people are in great difficulty when they start meditating. They come to me and they say, "This is something funny, strange. We never thought that there were so many thoughts." They have never closed their eyes, they have never sat in a relaxed posture, they have never gone in to see what was happening there because they were too engaged in the outside world, they were too occupied. Because of that occupation they never became aware of this constant activity inside.

In India, the ordinary waking consciousness is called the first state. The second state is that of dreaming. Any time you close your eyes you are in it. At night you are continuously in it, almost continuously. Whether you remember your dream in the morning or not is not of much importance, you go on dreaming. There are at least eight cycles of dreaming during the night. One cycle continues for many minutes—fifteen, twenty minutes; then there is a gap; then there is another cycle; then there is a gap; then again there is a cycle. Throughout the whole night you are continuously dreaming and dreaming and dreaming. This is the second state of consciousness.

This parable is concerned with the second state of consciousness. Ordinarily all desires exist in the second state of consciousness, the dreaming state. Desire is a dream and to work for a dream is doomed from the very beginning, because a dream can never become real. Even if sometimes you feel it has become almost real, it never becomes real—a dream by nature is empty. It has no substance in it.

The third state is sleep, deep sleep, *sushupti*. In it all dreaming disappears—but all consciousness also. While you are awake there is a little awareness, very little; when you are dreaming, even that little awareness disappears. But still there is an iota of awareness—that's why you can remember in the morning that you had a dream, such and such a dream. But in deep sleep even that disappears. It is as if you have completely disappeared. Nothing remains. A nothingness surrounds you.

These are the three ordinary states. The fourth state is called *turiya*. The fourth is simply called "the fourth." *Turiya* means "the fourth." The fourth state is that of a Buddha. It is almost like dreamless sleep with one difference—that difference is very great. It is as peaceful as deep sleep, as without dreams as deep sleep, but it is absolutely alert, aware.

Krishna says in his Gita that a real yogi never sleeps. That does not mean that a real yogi simply sits awake in his room the whole night. There are a few foolish people who are doing that. That a real yogi never sleeps means that while he is asleep he remains aware, alert.

Ananda lived with Buddha for forty years. He asked Buddha one day, "One thing surprises me very much; I am intrigued. You will have to answer me. This is just out of curiosity but I cannot contain it anymore. When you sleep at night I have watched you many times, for hours together, and you sleep in such a way that it seems as if you are awake. You sleep in such a graceful way; your face, your body—everything is so graceful. I have seen many other people sleeping, and they start mumbling, their faces go through contortions, their bodies lose all grace, their faces become ugly, they don't look beautiful anymore. . . ." All beauty has to be managed, controlled, practiced; in deep sleep it disappears. "And, one thing more," Ananda said. "You never change your posture, you remain in the same posture. Wherever you put your hand in the beginning, you keep it there the whole night. You never change it. It seems that deep down you are keeping absolutely alert." Buddha said, "You are right. That happens when meditation is perfect."

Then awareness penetrates your being so deeply that you are aware in all of the four states. When you are aware in all four states dreaming absolutely disappears, because in an alert mind a dream cannot exist. And the ordinary waking state becomes an extraordinary waking state—what Gurdjieff calls self-remembering. One remembers oneself absolutely, each moment. There is no gap. The remembrance is a continuity. Then one becomes a luminous being.

And deep sleep is there but its quality changes completely. The body is asleep but the soul is awake and alert, watchful. The whole body is deep in darkness but the lamp of inner consciousness burns bright.

This story says:

After many years of great poverty, which had never shaken his faith in God, he dreamed that someone bade him look for treasure under the bridge which leads to the king's palace in Prague.

After many years of great poverty it is natural that one should start dreaming about treasures. We always dream about that which we don't have. Fast for one day and in the night you will dream about food. Try to force celibacy upon yourself and your dreams will become sexual, they will have a quality of sexuality.

That's why psychoanalysis says that the analysis of dreams is of tremendous import, because it shows what you are repressing. Your dream becomes a symbolic indication of the repressed content of your mind. If a person continuously dreams about food, about feasts, that simply shows that the person is starving himself. Jaina monks always dream about food—they may say so, they may not. If you fast too much you are bound to dream about food. That's why many religious saints become so afraid of falling asleep.

Even Mahatma Gandhi was very afraid to go into sleep. He was trying to reduce it to as little as possible. Religious people make it a point to try not to sleep for too long—four hours, five hours at the most. Three is the ideal. Why? Because once your need of bodily rest is satisfied your mind starts weaving and spinning dreams. And immediately the mind brings up things which you have been repressing. Mahatma Gandhi said, "I have become a celibate as far as my waking consciousness is concerned, but in my dreams I am not a celibate." He was a true man in a sense—truer than other so-called saints. At least he accepted that in his dreams he was not yet celibate.

But unless you are celibate in your dreams you are not yet celibate, because the dream reveals whatsoever you are repressing during the day. The dream simply brings it back to your consciousness. Dreaming is a language, a communication from the unconscious which is saying, "Please don't do this to me. It is impossible to tolerate. Stop this nonsense. You are destroying my natural spontaneity. Allow me, allow whatsoever is potential in me to flower."

When a person represses nothing, dreams disappear. So a Buddha never dreams. If your meditation goes deep you will immediately find that your dreams are becoming less and less and less. The day your dreams completely disappear and you attain to clarity in your sleep—no clouds, no smoke, no thoughts; simple, silent sleep, without any interference of dreams—that day you have become a Buddha, your meditation has come to fruition.

Psychoanalysis insists that dreams have to be understood because man is very cunning: he can deceive while he is awake but
he cannot deceive when he is in a dream. A dream is truer . . .
Look at the irony. A dream is more true about you than your so-
called waking consciousness. Man has become so false, man has
become so fake that the waking consciousness cannot be relied
upon—you have corrupted it too much. A psychoanalyst immediately wants to go into your dreams, he does not want to know
about your religion, he does not want to know about your philosophy of life, he does not want to know whether you are a Hindu or
a Christian, an Indian or an American—that is all nonsense. He
wants to know what your dreams are. Look at the irony—your
dreams have become so real that your reality is less real than your
dreams. You are living such a pseudolife, inauthentic, false, that
the psychoanalyst has to go to your dreams to find a few glimpses
of truth. Only your dreams are still beyond your control.

There are people who try to control dreams also. In the East,
methods have been invented to control dreams. That means you are
not even allowing the unconscious to convey any message to you.
You can do that too. You can cultivate dreams if you work hard. You
can start planning your dreams. You can give a story to your own unconscious to unfold in your dreams. If you do it consistently, every
day, by and by you will be able to corrupt the unconscious.

For example, once a devotee of Krishna stayed with me. He
said, "I always dream of Krishna." I asked him, "How do you manage it? A dream is not something that you can manage. What
method have you tried?" He said, "A simple method which my
guru gave to me. Every night when I go to sleep, I go on thinking
and thinking about Krishna, fantasizing. After three years of continuously practicing fantasy while falling asleep, one day it happened. Whatsoever I had fantasized continued in my dream and it
became my dream. Since then I have been having tremendously
religious dreams."

I said, "You just go into the details—because you may have

managed the story but the unconscious will be sending messages in the story itself, the unconscious can use your story to send its messages." He said, "What do you mean?" I said, "You simply give me the content of your dream, the detailed content."

And he started telling me. It was absolutely sexual. Krishna was his lover and he had become a male gopi, a boyfriend. The content was homosexual. And they were dancing together and kissing and hugging and loving each other.

I said, "You have changed the figure, but the content still remains. And my understanding is that you are a homosexual." He was very much disturbed and shocked. He said, "What do you mean? How have you come to know about it?" I told him, "Your dream is a clear message."

He started weeping and crying. He said, "From my childhood I was never attracted to women, I was always attracted to men. And I thought that it was good because women would distract me from my path."

The homosexual content had entered into his religious story. Krishna was nothing but a homosexual partner. He became very disturbed and that very night the dream disappeared and a purely homosexual dream entered. He said, "What have you done to me?" I said, "I have not done anything. I have simply made your message clear to you. You can fabricate a story but that doesn't matter, the inner content remains the same."

Just see. Go to a person who is not religious. You will find nude pictures of women in Indian homes, in bachelors' homes. These people are not religious. But go to a religious man. He may have beautiful pictures of gods and goddesses but just look at the content, at the detail of it. Whether it is a film actress or whether it is a goddess makes no difference. Just look at the breasts! They will indicate exactly the same content. The story is different. Somebody has a picture of a goddess on his wall and somebody has Elizabeth Taylor or somebody else's picture, Sophia Loren—but it makes no difference. Whether you call her a goddess or you call her a film actress makes no difference. Look at the detail and you will see what that man is hankering after.

You can manipulate your dreams, you can destroy the purity of your unconscious's messages, but still the unconscious will go on giving you messages. It has to. It has to scream to you because you are destroying your own nature, your own spontaneity.

This dream happened

After many years of great poverty, which had never shaken his faith in God, he dreamed that someone bade him look for treasure under the bridge which leads to the king's palace in Prague.

Poor men always dream of kings' palaces and kings' treasure and things like that. If you have very rich dreams it simply shows that you are a poor man. Only very rich people dream of becoming monks, renunciates, sannyasins—a Buddha, a Mahavir. Living in their palaces they had dreams of becoming sannyasins, because they were fed up with their success. Success was finished for them, it had no charm, it had no allure, it had no fascination anymore. They thought now that a poor man's life is a real life and they started to seek somewhere else, somewhere they were not.

But the dream always goes somewhere else. The rich man thinks that the poor man is living a real life, and the poor man thinks that the rich man is living a real life. But the fallacy is the same: they both think, "Real life is somewhere else where I am not. Somehow I am always excluded from the real life—somebody else is enjoying it. Life is always happening somewhere else. Wherever I go, life simply disappears. Wherever I reach for it I always find emptiness." But it is always happening somewhere else. Life seems to be like the horizon, it is just ahead somewhere. It is a mirage.

When the dream recurred the third time he set out for Prague.

And remember, if a dream recurs too many times it almost starts looking real. Repetition makes things real.

Adolf Hitler wrote in his autobiography *Mein Kampf* that if you go on repeating a lie it becomes real. Repetition is the key. And he should know. He practiced it. He is not simply asserting something theoretical, he practiced it the whole of his life. He uttered lies, absolutely absurd lies, but one thing he insisted on—he went on repeating. When you go on repeating some lie again and again and again it starts becoming real, because the mind starts getting hypnotized by it.

Repetition is the method of hypnosis. Repeat anything and it becomes engraved in your being—that's how we are deluded in life. If you repeat, "This woman is beautiful, this woman is beautiful," if you go on repeating it, you will start seeing beauty in her. It may be there, it may not be there, it doesn't matter—if you repeat it long enough it will become true. If you think that money is the goal of life, go on repeating it and it will become your goal of life.

That's how all advertising functions: it just goes on repeating. The advertiser believes in the science of repetition; he simply goes on repeating that this brand of cigarette is the best. When you read it for the first time you may not believe it. But next time, again and again—how long can you remain an unbeliever? By and by the belief will arise. And the belief will be such that you may not even become conscious of it. It will be subliminal, it will be just underneath consciousness. One day suddenly, when you go to the store and the storekeeper asks what brand of cigarette you need, you will say a certain brand. That repetition worked. It hypnotized you.

That's how religions have been functioning in the world—and all politics depends on it too. Advertise, go on repeating to the public, and don't be bothered whether they believe or not—that's not the point. Hitler says there is only one difference between a truth and a lie: the truth is a lie that has been repeated very often. And man can believe any lies. Man's gullibility is infinite. Man can believe in hell, man can believe in heaven, man can believe in angels, man can believe in devils, man can believe in anything! You just go on repeating.

And there is no need to argue. An advertisement never argues—have you observed the fact? There is no need to argue. The advertisement simply persuades you, it never argues. An arguer may not be able to convince you but a person who persuades you, who simply goes on throwing soft suggestions at you, not direct arguments . . . Because when somebody argues with you, you may become defensive, but if somebody simply goes on hinting at certain things, not in any direct way, just supposing, you are more prone to be convinced by it.

Dreaming functions in that way; a dream is a salesman. A dream simply goes on repeating itself. It never argues, it simply insists on being repeated. And, often repeated, one starts believing in it.

When it happened thrice he set out for Prague. But the bridge was guarded day and night and he did not dare start digging.

In the world there is much competition. Every place is guarded and every object has to be fought for—it is not easy. This

is something very strange. In this world nothing is meaningful
and yet for everything you have to fight. Nothing seems to be significant but there is much competition, much conflict. Everybody
is rushing toward it, that creates the trouble—it is not that there is
something in it. There is nothing in it but everybody is trying to
rush toward it. Everybody is hankering for everybody else's place,
that's why the world is so crowded.

In fact, it is not as crowded as it seems. Look . . . we are sitting
here, everybody is sitting in his own place. This place is not
crowded at all. But if a frenzy suddenly takes hold of your mind
and everybody starts trying to reach another's place, then this
place would be crowded. Right now you are sitting religiously; in
that situation you would be rushing at each other politically. Right
now you are satisfied with your place and you are not hankering
for anybody's place—at least not in Chuang Tzu auditorium. But if
you start pushing yourself into others' places, others will become
defensive, they will start pushing you. A fight, a war, will ensue.

Why are there so many wars in the world? The reason is that
everybody is trying to have another's territory. And the other may
be trying the same thing. He may be looking at you.

But the bridge was guarded day and night and he did not dare
start digging. Nevertheless he went to the bridge every
morning and kept walking around it until evening.

That's what many people are doing. Very few succeed, many
simply walk around. But they go on doing it. Even if you cannot succeed, your desires, your hopes, are continuously there. At least you
can go to the place, near the palace, and you can walk around. The
whole day, from morning to evening he was walking around—that's

what many people are doing, waiting for some miracle to happen. Someday there may be no guards, someday may be a holiday, someday there may be a possibility to dig . . . one waits and one goes on waiting. It never happens but one's whole life is wasted in waiting.

Nevertheless he went to the bridge every morning and kept walking around it until evening. Finally, the captain of the guards, who had been watching him, asked in a kindly way whether he was looking for something or waiting for somebody. Rabbi Eisik told him of the dream which had brought him here from a faraway country. The captain laughed: "And so to please the dream, you poor fellow wore out your shoes to come here! As for having faith in dreams, if I had had it, I should have had to get going when a dream once told me to go to Cracow and dig for treasure under the stove in the room of a Jew—Eisik, son of Yekel, that was the name! Eisik, son of Yekel! I can just imagine what it would be like, how I should have to try every house over there, where one half of the Jews are named Eisik, and the other Yekel!" And he laughed again. Rabbi Eisik bowed, traveled home, dug up the treasure from under the stove, and built the house of prayer which is called "Reb Eisik's Shul."

It is a beautiful story—and very true. That is how it is happening in life. You are looking somewhere else for that which is already there within you.

Rabbi Eisik bowed, thanked the man, traveled home. . . . This is the journey of religion: traveling back home. And a man who has understood life always pays his respects toward life because it has shocked him out of his dreams. He is not against life; he simply knows that he has nothing to do with life, he simply knows that he was searching in a wrong direction.

Life has always been compassionate, life has been telling you again and again that you can find nothing here—go back home. But you don't listen.

You earn money, and one day money is there—then life says to you, "What have you got?" But you don't listen. Now you think you have to put your money into politics, you have to become a prime minister or a president—then everything will be okay. One day you are a prime minister, and life again says, "What have you got?" You don't listen. You go on thinking of something else and something else and something else. Life is vast—that's why many lives are wasted.

But don't be angry at life. It is not life that is frustrating you, it is you who are not listening to life. And this I call a criterion, a touchstone: if you see a saint who is against life, bitter against life, know well he has not understood yet. Otherwise he will bow down to life in deep respect and reverence, because life has awakened him out of his dreams. Life is very shocking, that's why. Life is painful. The pain comes because you are desiring something which is not possible. It doesn't come from life, it comes from your expectation.

People say that man proposes and God disposes. It has never happened. God has never disposed of anything. But in your own proposition you have disposed of something yourself. Listen to God's proposition, keep your own proposition to yourself. Keep quiet. Listen to what the whole is willing—don't try to have your private goals, don't try to have your private desires. Don't ask anything individually—the whole is moving toward its destiny. You simply be part of it. Cooperate. Don't be in a conflict. Surrender to it. And life always sends you back to your own reality—that is why it is shocking.

It shocks you because it doesn't fulfill your dreams. And it is

good that life never fulfills your dreams—it always goes on dispos-
ing, in a way. It gives you a thousand and one opportunities to be
frustrated so that you can understand that expectations are not
good and dreams are futile and desires are never fulfilled. Then
you drop desiring, you drop dreaming, you drop proposing. Suddenly you are back home and the treasure is there.

Rabbi Eisik bowed, traveled home, dug up the treasure from
under his stove, and built the house of prayer which is called
"Reb Eisik's Shul."

The treasure had always been waiting there under his
stove. In the same room he dreamed that the treasure was somewhere near the palace of the king in Prague. In his own room, in
his own house, it was just there waiting to be dug up.

This is very indicative. Your treasure is in your own being—
don't look for it somewhere else. All palaces and all bridges to the
palace are meaningless; you have to create your own bridge within
your own being. The palace is there; the treasure is there.

God never sends anybody into this world without a treasure. He
sends you ready for every situation—how can it be otherwise?
When a father sends his son on a long journey he makes every
preparation. Even for unexpected situations the father provides.
He makes all provisions. You are carrying everything that you
need. Just go into the seeker and don't go seeking outside. Seek
the seeker, let the seeker be the sought.

Because of this, Rabbi Eisik built the house of prayer. It was
such a tremendous revelation, such a tremendous experience—
"God has put the treasure where I have always lived. I was poor because of myself, I was not poor because God wanted me to be poor.

As far as he is concerned I was a king, always a king." Because of this understanding he made a prayer house, a temple, out of this treasure. He used it well.

Whenever somebody comes to his innermost treasure, prayer arises—that is the meaning of the story. He made a house of prayer called Reb Eisik's Shul. Whenever you understand the grace of God, the compassion, the love, what else can you do? A great prayer of thankfulness rises into your being, you feel so overpowered by his love, overwhelmed. What else can you do? You simply bow down and you pray.

And remember, if you pray to ask for something, it is not prayer. When you pray to thank him for something, only then is it prayer. Prayer is always a thanksgiving. If you ask for something then the prayer is still corrupted by desire. Then it is not prayer yet—it is still poisoned by dreaming. Real prayer happens only when you have attained to yourself, when you have known what God has given to you already without your asking for it. When you realize what you have been given, what infinite sources have been given to you, a prayer arises. You would like to say to God, "Thank you." There is nothing else in it but a pure thank-you.

When a prayer is just a thank-you it is a prayer. Never ask for anything in a prayer; never say, "Do this, do that; don't do this, don't do that." Never advise God. That shows your irreligiousness, that shows your lack of trust. Thank him. Your life is already a benediction, a blessing. Each moment is such pure joy, but you are missing it, that I know. That's why the prayer is not arising—otherwise you would build a house of prayer; your whole life would become that house of prayer; you would become that temple—his shrine. His shrine would burst from your being. He would flower in you and his fragrance would spread to the winds.

It does not happen because you are missing something. And you are missing not because of him, you are missing because of yourself. If you desire, and you think that the treasure is somewhere else, you move into the future. The future is needed because you desire; the future is a by-product of desiring. How can you project desire in the present? The present is already here, you cannot project any desire in it, it does not allow desire. If you desire, the present has already gone; you can desire only in the future, only in the tomorrow.

This has to be understood. Desire is always in the future but the future is never there. The future is that which is not, and desire is only in the future. And desire comes out of the past which also is not. The past is gone and the future has not yet come. Desire comes out of the past because you must have known what you desire in the past somehow. How can you desire something which is absolutely new? You cannot desire the new. You can only ask for a repetition. You had some money, you will ask for more—but money you know. You had some power, you ask for more—but power you know. Man cannot desire the unknown. Desire is just a repetition of the known. Just look at it. You have known it and you are not fulfilled, so you are asking for it again. Do you think you will be fulfilled? At the most you can ask for more quantity, but if one rupee is not fulfilling, how can a thousand rupees be fulfilling? If one rupee is unfulfilling, ten thousand rupees will be ten thousandfold more unfulfilling—that is simple logic. If one woman has not fulfilled you, then ten thousand women are not going to fulfill you. If one woman has created such a hell then ten thousand women . . . just think! It is simple arithmetic. You can solve it.

You can ask only out of the past and into the future and both are nonexistential. That which exists is the present. This very moment is the only moment there is. You cannot desire in it, you can just be in it. You can just enjoy it.

And I have never come across a person who can be miserable in the present. You will be surprised. Many times people come to me and they say that they are very miserable and this and that, and I say to them, "Close your eyes and find out right now whether you are miserable or not." They close their eyes, then they open their eyes, and they say, "Right now I am not miserable."

Right now nobody is miserable. There is no possibility. It is not allowed by the nature of things. This very moment are you miserable? This very moment? You may have been miserable a moment before, okay—that is right. Or you may be miserable a moment afterward—that too is allowed. But this very moment, between these two nonexistential moments, are you miserable? Nobody has ever been.

This moment is always pure benediction; this moment is always one of joy, of tremendous delight; this moment is God's moment. The past is yours, the future is yours, the present is God's. We divide time into three tenses—past, present, future—but we should not divide it in that way. That division is not right. Time can be divided between the past and the future but the present is not part of time, it is part of eternity. God has no past, remember, you cannot say God was. God has no future—you cannot say God will be. God has only one tense—present. God is. God always is. In fact, God is only another name for the "isness" of existence. Whenever you are also in the moment, whenever you are also in this "isness," you are happy, blessed. A prayer arises. You become a shrine. You will become Reb Eisik's Shul, you will become a prayer house.

"Take this story to heart," Rabbi Bunam used to add, "and make what it says your own: There is something you cannot find anywhere in the world, not even at the Zaddik's, and there is, nevertheless, a place where you can find it."

"Zaddik" means the Master. The word "zaddik" comes from a Hebrew root which means: the pure, the purest, purity itself. The Zaddik means the Master—who has attained to his "presentness,"

who is no longer in the past and no longer in the future, who is just herenow, who is just a presence. To be in the presence of a Master is to be in the presence of a presence. That's all. And to be in the presence of a Master can help you to be present because his presence can become infectious.

But Rabbi Bunam says, "There *is* something you cannot find anywhere in the world, not even at the Zaddik's . . ." He says that there is something which you cannot find anywhere, not even in the presence of a Master. But don't feel hopeless—there is nevertheless a place where you can find it.

That place is you, and that time is now. In fact, the Zaddik's, the Master's, effort is nothing but to throw you to your "presentness," to make you available to God, or, to make God available to you.

This "presentness" cannot be taught but it can be caught— hence the value of *satsang*, of being in the presence of a Zaddik, of a Master, of a guru. Just to be there doing nothing . . . In fact, a Master is not doing anything. He is just there. A Master is a prayer, a constant thankfulness. With each breath he is thanking God— not verbally, his very breathing is a thankfulness; with each beat of his heart he goes on saying "thank you." His thank-you is not verbal, it is existential. His being is prayer. To be in the presence of such a man may help you to have some taste of prayer. That taste will start a new journey in your life—the inward journey.

You have been seeking for centuries, for millennia, and you have not yet found. Now, let the seeker be the sought. You have traveled outside for so long that you are very tired, very exhausted.

Jesus says, "Those who are tired, those whose burden is heavy, they should come to me. I will give them rest." What does he mean? He simply means, "Come to me. I am at rest. Be close to me. Have a taste of it." And that very taste will turn the tide and you will start moving inward.

You are here with me. Have a taste of my being. Don't just listen to my words, listen to me. Taste me. And then suddenly you will be here and now, and you will be turning inward and you will

not ask for anything and you will not desire anything and you will
not have any movement into the future and you will not have any
clinging with the past.

And then this moment is liberation, this moment is enlightenment.

Enough for today.

Neither Do I Condemn Thee

The angry crowd and the
adulterous woman

On the
difference
between
morality and
religiousness

John 8

1. Jesus went unto the Mount of Olives.

2. And early in the morning he came again into the temple,
   and all the people came unto him; and he sat down, and
   taught them.

3. And the scribes and Pharisees brought unto him a woman
   taken in adultery; and when they had set her in their midst,

4. They said unto him, master, this woman was taken in
   adultery, in the very act.

5. Now Moses in the law commanded us, that such should be stoned: but what sayest thou?

6. This they said, tempting him, that they might have to accuse him. But Jesus stooped down, and with his finger wrote on the ground, as though he heard them not.

7. So when they continued asking him, he lifted up himself, and said unto them, he that is without sin among you, let him first cast a stone at her.

8. And again he stooped down, and wrote on the ground.

9. And they which heard it, being convicted by their own conscience, went out one by one, beginning at the eldest, even unto the last: and Jesus was left alone, and the woman standing in the midst.

10. When Jesus had lifted up himself, and saw none but the woman, he said unto her, woman, where are those thine accusers? Hath no man condemned thee?

11. She said, no man, lord. And Jesus said unto her, neither do I condemn thee: Go, and sin no more.

Religion always deteriorates into morality. Morality is dead religion. Religion is alive morality. They never meet, they cannot meet because life and death never meet; light and darkness never meet. But the problem is that they look very alike—the corpse looks very like the living man. Everything is just like when the man was alive: the same face, the same eyes, the same nose, the hair, the body. Just one thing is missing, and that one thing is invisible.

Life is missing, but life is not tangible and not visible. So when a man is dead, he looks as if he is still alive. And with the problem of morality, it becomes more complex.

Morality looks exactly like religion, but it is not. It is a corpse: it stinks of death. Religion is youth, religion is freshness—the freshness of the flowers and the freshness of the morning dew. Religion is splendor—the splendor of the stars, of life, of existence itself. When religion is there, there is no morality at all and the person is moral. But there is no morality; there is no idea of what morality is. It is just natural; it follows you as your shadow follows you. You need not carry your shadow, you need not think about your shadow. You need not look back again and again and see whether the shadow is following you still or not. It follows.

Just like that, morality follows a religious person. He never considers it, he never deliberately thinks about it; it is his natural flavor. But when religion is dead, when life has disappeared, then one starts thinking about morality continuously. Consciousness has disappeared, and conscience becomes the only shelter.

Conscience is a pseudo phenomenon. Consciousness is yours, conscience is borrowed. Conscience is of the society, of the collective mind; it does not arise in your own being. When you are conscious you act rightly because your act is conscious, and the conscious act can never go wrong. When your eyes are fully open and there is light, you don't try to get through the wall, you go through the door. When there is no light and your eyes are also not functioning well, naturally you grope in the dark. You have to think a thousand and one times where the door is—"To the left, to the right? Am I moving in the right direction?" And you stumble upon the furniture, and you try to get out through the wall.

A religious person is one who has eyes to see, who has awareness. In that awareness actions are naturally good. Let me repeat: naturally good. Not that you manage them to be good. Managed goodness is not goodness at all. It is pseudo, it is pretension, it is hypocrisy. When goodness is natural, spontaneous, just as trees are green and the sky is blue, so is the religious man moral—completely unaware of his morality. Aware of himself but unaware of his morality, he has no idea that he is moral, that he is good, that what he is doing is right. Out of his awareness comes innocence, out of his awareness comes the right act—of its own accord. It has not to be brought, it has not to be cultivated, it has not to be practiced. Then morality has a beauty, but it is no more morality; it is simply moral. In fact, it is just a religious way of living.

But when religion has disappeared, then you have to manage it. Then you have to constantly think about what is right and what is wrong. And how are you going to decide what is right and what is wrong? You don't have your own eyes to see, you don't have your own heart to feel. You are dead and dull. You don't have your own intelligence to go into matters, then you have to depend on the collective mind that surrounds you.

Religiousness has one flavor—whether you are Christian or Hindu or Mohammedan does not make any difference. A religious person is simply religious. He is neither Hindu nor Mohammedan nor Christian. But a moral person is not just moral. Either he is Hindu or Christian or Mohammedan or Buddhist, because morality has to be learned from the outside. If you are born in a Buddhist country, in a Buddhist society, you will learn the Buddhist morality. If you are born in a Christian world, you will learn the Christian morality. You will learn from others. And you *have* to learn from others because you don't have your own insight. So morality is borrowed; it is social, it is mob—it comes from the masses.

And from where does it come to the masses? From tradition. They have heard what is right and what is wrong, and they have carried it down the ages. It is being given from one generation to another. Nobody bothers whether it is a corpse, nobody bothers whether the heart beats still; it goes on being given from one generation to another. It is dull, dead, heavy; it kills joy, it is a killjoy.

It kills celebration, it kills laughter, it makes people ugly, it makes people heavy, monotonous, boring. But it has a long tradition.

Another thing to be remembered: religion is always born anew. In Jesus, religion is born again. It is not the same religion that was with Moses. It has not come from Moses. It has no continuity with the past; it is utterly discontinuous with the past.

It arises again and again just like a flower comes on the rosebush. It has nothing to do with the flowers that had come before on the rosebush. It is discontinuous. It comes on its own; it has no past, no history, no biography. For the moment it is there, and for the moment it is so beautifully there, so authentically there. For the moment it is so strong, so alive, and yet so fragile. In the morning sun it was so young . . . by the evening it will be gone, the petals will start falling down into the earth from which they had come in the first place. And it will not leave any trace behind: if you come the next day, it is no longer there. And it has not left any marks; it has simply disappeared. As it has come out of nothingness, so it has gone back to nothingness, to the original source.

Just like that is religion. When it happens in a Buddha, it is fresh, young like a rose flower. Then it disappears, it leaves no traces. Buddha has said "Religion is like a bird flying in the sky, it leaves no footmarks." Then it happens in a Moses—it is fresh, young again. Then in Jesus—it is fresh and young again. And when it will happen to you, it will not have any continuity, it will not come from somebody else—Christ, Buddha, me; it will not come from anybody else. It will *arise* in you, it will bloom in you. It will be a flowering of your being, and then it will be gone. You cannot give it to anybody; it is not transferable. It cannot be given, cannot be borrowed; it is not a thing.

Yes, if somebody wants to learn, it can be learned. If somebody wants to imbibe, it can be imbibed. When a disciple learns around a Master, absorbs the vibes of the Master, then too it is something that is happening within him. Maybe he gets the challenge, the provocation, the call from the outside, but that which arises,

arises in him, utterly in him; it does not come from the outside. It may be like you are not aware that you can sing; you have never tried, you have never thought about the possibility. Then one day you see a singer, and suddenly his song starts pulsating around you, and in a moment of awakening you become aware that you have also got a throat and a heart. And now, suddenly, for the first time, you become also aware that there has been a song hidden in you, and you release it. But the song comes from your innermost core; it arises from your being. Maybe the provocation, the call came from the outside, but not the song.

So the Master is a catalytic agent. His presence provokes something in you; his presence does not function as a cause.

C. G. Jung is right in bringing a new concept to the Western world. It has existed in the East for centuries—the concept of synchronicity. There are things that happen as cause and effect, and there are things that don't happen as cause and effect, but just by synchronicity. This idea has to be understood, because this idea will help you to understand the difference between morality and religion.

Morality is cause and effect. Your father and your mother have taught you something: they function as the cause, and then the effect goes on continuing in you. Then you will teach your children: you will become the cause, and the effect will continue in your children. But listening to a singer, suddenly you start humming a tune. There is no cause-and-effect relationship. The singer is not the cause, and you are not the effect. You have caused the effect yourself—you are both the cause and the effect. The singer functioned only as a remembrance; the singer functioned only as a catalytic agent.

What has happened to me I cannot give to you. Not that I don't want to give it to you, no—because it cannot be given, its very nature is such that it cannot be given—but I can present it to you, I can make it available to you. Seeing that it is possible, seeing that it has happened to another man, "Why not to me?" suddenly something clicks inside you, you become alert to a possibility, alert to a door that is in you but you were never looking at, you had forgotten it. And something starts sprouting in you.

I function as a catalytic agent not as a cause. The concept of synchronicity simply says that one thing can start something somewhere without it being a cause. It says that if somebody plays sitar in a room where another sitar has been placed in the corner, and if the player is really a master, a maestro, the sitar that is just sitting there in the corner will start throbbing—because of the other sitar being played in the room, the vibe, the whole milieu. And the sitar that is just sitting there in the corner—nobody is playing it, nobody is touching it—you can see its strings vibrating, whispering. Something that is hidden is surfacing, something that was not manifest is manifesting.

Religion is synchronicity; morality is causal. Morality comes from the outside, religion arises in you. When religion disappears there is only morality, and morality is very dangerous.

First, you don't know yourself what is right, but you start pretending: the hypocrite is created. You start pretending, you start showing that whatsoever you are doing is right. You don't know what right is, and naturally, because you don't know you can only pretend. From the back door you will continue doing the same: that you *know* it is right. From the back door you will have one life, from the front door, another. From the front door you may be smiling, and from the back door you may be crying and weeping. From the front door you will pretend to be a saint, and from the back door you will be as much of a sinner as anybody else. Your life will become split. This is what is creating schizophrenia in the whole human consciousness. You become two, or many.

Naturally when you are two, there is constant conflict. Naturally when you are many, there is a crowd and much noise, and you can never settle in silence, you can never rest in silence. Silence is possible only when you are one, when there is nobody else within you, when you are one piece—not fragmented.

Morality creates schizophrenia, split personalities, divisions. A moral person is not an individual because he is divided. Only a religious person is an individual. The moral person has a personality but no individuality. Personality means *persona,* mask. And he has many personalities, not just one, because he has to have many personalities around him. In different situations, different personalities are needed. With different people, different personalities are needed. To one he shows one face, to another he shows another face. One goes on changing faces.

Watch, and you will see how you go on changing faces every moment. Alone you have one face. In your bathroom you have one face, in the office you have another. Have you observed the fact that in your bathroom you become more childish? Sometimes you can show your tongue to yourself in the mirror, or you can make faces, or you can hum a tune, sing a song, or you can even have a little dance in the bathroom. But while you are dancing or showing your tongue in the mirror, if you become aware that your child is looking through the keyhole, you change—immediate change! The old face comes back . . . the father personality. "This cannot be done in front of the child" otherwise what will he think? That you are also like him? So what about that seriousness that you show to him always? You immediately pull down another face; you become serious. The song disappears, the dance disappears, the tongue disappears. You are back into your so-called front-door personality.

Morality creates conflict in you because it creates many faces. And the problem is that when you have many faces, you tend to forget which is your original one. With so many faces how can you remember which is your original one?

The Zen Masters say the first thing for a seeker to know is his original face, because only then can something start. Only the original face can grow, a mask cannot grow. A false face can have no growth. Growth is possible only for the original face, because only the original has life.

So the first thing is to know "What is my original face?" and it is arduous, because there is a long queue of false faces, and you are lost in your false faces. And sometimes you may think "This is my original face." If you go deep into it, you will find this again is a false face, maybe it is more ancient than the others, so it looks more original.

The Zen Masters say, if you really want to see your original face, you will have to go before birth, you will have to conceive of what your face was before you were born, or what your face will be when you are dead.

Between birth and death you have all kinds of false faces. Even a small child starts learning the pseudo tricks, diplomacies. Just a small child—maybe one day old, just out of the womb—starts learning, because he sees that if he smiles, then the mother feels very good. If he smiles the mother immediately gives her breast to him. If he smiles, the mother comes close, hugs him, pats him. He has learned a trick, that if he wants the mother to be close to him, if he wants to be hugged and kissed and talked to, he has to smile. Now the diplomat is born, the politician is born. Whenever he wants the mother to pull him close . . . He cannot call, he cannot talk, but he can wait until she looks at him then he can smile. The moment he smiles, the mother comes running. Now whether he feels like smiling in this moment is not the point, he wants the mother, he wants to manipulate the mother. He has a trick, a strategy, a technique that he has learned: smile, and mother comes. Then he will go on smiling, and whenever he wants somebody to come close, he will smile. And this face will not be the true face.

Your smiles are not true. Your tears are also not true. Your whole personality is synthetic, plastic. The moral person, the so-called moralist, has many personalities but no individuality. The religious person has individuality but no personality. He is one. His taste is always one.

Buddha is reported to have said, taste me from anywhere and

you will find the same taste as when you taste the sea. From this side, from that side, from this shore, from that shore—taste the sea from anywhere and it is salty. And Buddha says, so is my taste. Taste me while I am asleep, taste me while I am awake, taste me when somebody is insulting me, taste me when somebody is praising me—you will always find the same taste, the taste of a Buddha.

The religious person is an individual.

The second thing to be remembered: the moralist is always making efforts to impose his morality on others—for many reasons. First: he uses his morality to manipulate himself. Naturally, he does the same to others; he starts using his morality to manipulate others. He uses morality for his own strategies, diplomacies. Naturally, he learns a trick: that if he can enforce his morality on others, then things will be easier.

For example, if the moralist speaks the truth, his truth is not very deep. Deep down there are only lies and lies. But at least in society he pretends to speak the truth. He will try to impose his truth on others also. He would like everybody else to speak the truth, because he will be very much afraid that if somebody lies and tricks him, deceives him . . . And he knows that he himself is lying and deceiving people in subtle words, but on the surface he keeps the truth. And he goes on shouting "Everybody should be true!" He is very much afraid. He knows that just as he is deceiving others, others may be deceiving him.

Bertrand Russell has said that thieves are always against stealing. A thief has to be against stealing; otherwise somebody will steal things from him. And he has been making so much effort to steal things from others that if others steal things from him, then what will be the point? A thief will always shout "Stealing is bad! Never steal! You will be thrown into hell!" So nobody steals, then the thief is free to steal.

If nobody speaks untruths, then you can speak untruths and exploit people easily. If everybody speaks untruths, how can you exploit? Just think: a society where everybody speaks untruths, and it is an accepted phenomenon that everybody tells lies. Then you will be at a loss—you will not be able to cheat people. Whatsoever you say, people will think you are a liar—"Everybody tells lies here"; nobody can be deceived. So, in his own interest, the liar has to go on preaching morality. "Speak the truth, never steal, do this, do that"—and from the back door he goes on doing just the opposite. This has to be understood.

If somebody's pocket is picked right now—somebody steals—then many will be there shouting, "Catch the thief! Kill the thief! Who is there?" And many will shout. Remember, the shouters are just showing one thing: that they are also thieves. By shouting they are showing many things. One thing is: "Remember, I am not the thief, because I am so much against. Nobody should ever think or suspect me because I am against all of this kind of thing. I am a moral person." Those who are pickpockets will shout more, and if the real pickpocket is caught, then the pickpockets will beat him to show everybody that they are very much against it.

This is a very, very complex phenomenon. A religious person is a totally different person. He will be able to forgive, he will be able to understand. He will be able to see the limitations of man and the problems of man. He will not be so hard and so cruel—he cannot be. His compassion will be infinite.

Before we enter into these sutras, a few things have to be understood.

First: the concept of sin, the concept of the immoral act. What is immoral? How should we define immorality? And what is the criterion? One thing is immoral in India, another thing is immoral in China. That which is immoral in India may be moral in Iran, and that which is moral in Russia may be immoral in India. There are a thousand and one moralities. How to decide? Because now that the world has become a global village, there is much confusion. What is right?

To eat meat is right? Is it moral or immoral? The vegetarian says it is immoral. Many Jains have come to me many times and said, "What about Jesus eating meat? How can Jesus be an enlightened person—and you say that he is enlightened—how can he be an enlightened person? He eats meat." For a Jain it is impossible to conceive that Jesus can be enlightened although he eats meat. Jains have come to me and said to me, "How can Ramakrishna be enlightened? He eats fish. He cannot be." Now they have a very definite criterion with them—vegetarianism.

One Jain monk was talking to me, and he said, "I cannot believe that Jesus or Ramakrishna are enlightened, they eat meat."

I told him, "Do you know that there are people in the world who think that to drink milk is almost like eating meat? Because it is an animal food. Now, milk is an animal food. It is almost like blood because it comes out of the mother's blood. It is also full of live bacteria. There are people in the world, real fanatics, who take things to the very extreme. They say that milk, cheese, and butter are all animal foods—they have to be avoided."

I asked the Jain monk, "Mahavir used to drink milk. What do you say? He was drinking an animal food. Was he enlightened or not? Now Indian scriptures say milk is the purest food—sattvika—the purest food is milk. It is not. It is an animal food!"

That Jain monk started perspiring when he heard that milk is an animal food. And he said, "What are you talking about? Milk is the sattvik food, the purest food!"

But I said, "This is the analysis, the scientific analysis. Prove it wrong. That's why when you drink too much milk your face starts becoming red: milk creates blood—it becomes blood in you. That's why milk is so vital. And milk is a hundred percent food, that's why children live only on milk. It supplies everything. It becomes blood, it becomes your flesh, it becomes your skin, your bone, your marrow; it becomes everything. It is pure animal food. Now how to decide who is right?"

There are a thousand and one moralities. If you go on deciding, you will be in difficulty; it will be impossible for you. You will go mad, you will not be able to eat, you will not be able to sleep, you will not be able to do anything!

Now, there is a Jain sect that is afraid of breathing. To breathe is immoral, because with each breath you kill many, many small cells living around you in the air. They are true. That's why the doctor has to use a mask, so that he does not go on inhaling things which are moving around—infections. That Jain sect is afraid to breathe. Breathing becomes immoral.

Walking becomes immoral—there are Jains who don't walk in the night because they may kill something, an ant or something, in the darkness. Mahavir never moved in the night, never moved in the rainy season because then there are many more insects around. Movement becomes difficult, breathing becomes difficult. If you go on looking around at all the moralities, you will simply go crazy or you will have to commit suicide. But to commit suicide is immoral!

If you listen to all kinds of moralities that seems to be the logical thing: just commit suicide. That seems to be the least immoral thing. One act and you are finished, then there will be no immorality. But that too is immoral. And when you commit suicide you are not dying alone, remember. It is not killing one person. You have millions of cells in the body that are alive, millions of lives inside you, which will die with you. So you have killed millions of people. When you fast, is it moral or immoral?

There arc people who say to fast is moral, and there are people who say to fast is immoral. Why? Because when you fast you kill many cells inside, because they die of starvation. If you fast, then one kilo in weight disappears every day. You are killing many things inside you. One kilo in weight disappears every day. Within a month you will be just a structure of bones. All those people who used to live inside you—small people—they have all died. You have killed all of them.

Or there are people who say to fast is like eating meat. . . . Very strange. And that is true, there is a logic to it. When one kilo in weight disappears, where has it gone? You have eaten it! Your body

needs that kind of food every day. You go on replacing it with outside food. If you don't replace it with outside food . . . the body
goes on eating because the body needs; for twenty-four hours, the
body has to live. It needs a certain fuel. Then it starts eating its
own flesh. To be on a fast is to be a cannibal.

These moralities can drive you mad! There is no way to choose.
Then what is moral to me? To be aware is moral. What you are doing is not the question. If you are doing it in full awareness, then
whatsoever it is—it is irrelevant what it is—irrespective of the fact
of what it is, if you are doing in full awareness, it is moral. If you
are doing unawares, unconscious, then it is immoral.

To me, morality means awareness.

The French language seems to be the only language that has
only one word for two words: "conscience" and "consciousness."
That seems to be very, very beautiful. Consciousness is conscience. Ordinarily, consciousness is one thing and conscience is
another thing. Consciousness is yours. Conscience is given to you
by others; it is a conditioning.

Live by consciousness, become more and more conscious, and
you will become more and more moral—and you will not become
a moralist. You will become moral, and you will not become a
moralist. The moralist is an ugly phenomenon.

Now the sutras:

Jesus went unto the Mount of Olives. . . .

He always used to go to the mountains whenever he would
feel that his consciousness was becoming dusty, his mirror was

covered with dust. He would go to the mountains in aloneness to cleanse his being, to cleanse his consciousness. It is like you take a bath, and after the bath you feel the body is fresh, young.

Meditation is like an inner bath. To be alone for a few moments every day is a must; otherwise you will gather too much dust, and because of that dust your mirror will not reflect anymore, or will not reflect rightly. It may start distorting things.

Have you not watched? A single dust particle goes in your eye, and your vision becomes distorted. The same is true about the inner vision—the inner eye—so much dust goes on collecting, and dust comes from relationship. Just as when you travel on a dusty road, you collect dust; when you move with people who are dusty, you collect dust. They are all throwing their dust all around, they are all throwing wrong vibes—and they cannot do anything, they are helpless. I am not saying that you condemn them. What can they do?

If you go to a hospital and everybody is ill in the hospital, and if they are throwing their infections all around—they can't help it. They breathe and the infection goes out. Have you not seen it when you go to the hospital to visit somebody? Just one hour in the hospital and you start feeling a kind of sickness, and you had come perfectly healthy? Just the smell of the hospital, just the faces of the nurses and the doctors, and the medical instruments, and that particular hospital smell, and people who are all ill, and the whole vibe of illness and death always there . . . somebody is always dying.

Just one hour there and you feel very low; a kind of nausea arises in you.

Coming out of the hospital you feel a great relief. The same is the situation in the world. You don't know because you live in the world. The nurse who goes on working in the hospital, and the doctor who goes on working in the hospital—they have to become insensitive; otherwise they would die, they would not be able to live there. They have become insensitive; they go on moving.

That's why many times you see doctors looking very, very insensitive—that is their protection. The patient goes on saying that this is wrong and that is wrong, and the doctor stands there almost not listening. The relatives of the patient go on running after the doctor and go on telling him that this is going wrong and that is. . . . And he says, "Everything will be okay. I will come tomorrow morning. When I come on my round, I will see." Now you are feeling so concerned, and he seems to be absolutely unconcerned. This is just to protect himself. If he becomes too sensitive, he will not be able to survive. He has to become hard, he has to create a kind of stoniness around himself. That stoniness will protect him—will protect him from the hospital and the patients and the whole atmosphere. Doctors become hard, insensitive; nurses become hard, insensitive.

The same is happening in the world at large. It is a kind of big hospital, because everybody is ill here and everybody is on the deathbed; and everybody is full of anger and violence and aggression and jealousy and possessiveness; and everybody is false, pseudo, and everybody is a hypocrite—this is the world. You don't feel it, but when a Jesus moves among you, he feels it because he comes from the heights. He descends from the mountains.

If you go to the Himalayas and after living a few days in the Himalayan freshness you come back to the plains, then you feel how dusty, how ugly, how heavy the vibe is. Now you have comparison. You have seen the fresh waters of the Himalayas—those fresh fountains running forever, and the crystal-clear water—and then the municipal tap water. You have the comparison then. Only a meditator knows that the world is ill, only a meditator feels that everything is wrong here. And when a meditator moves amid you, naturally he feels much more dust collecting on himself than you can feel, because you have lost all sensitivity.

You have forgotten that you are a mirror! You know that you are just a dust collector. Only a meditator knows that he is a mirror.

So Jesus goes again and again to the mountains.

Jesus went unto the Mount of Olives. And early in the
morning he came again into the temple, and all the people
came unto him; and he sat down, and taught them.

You can come into the temple only when you have been to the
mountains—and that does not mean that you really have to go to
the mountains. It is not an outer phenomenon. The mountain is
within you. If you can be alone, if you can forget the whole world
for a few seconds, you will regain your freshness. And only then
can you go to the temple, because only then *are* you a temple. And
only then will your presence in the temple be a real presence; and
there will be a harmony between you and the temple. Remember,
unless you bring your temple to the temple, there is no temple. If
you simply go to the temple, and don't bring your temple there
within you, it is just a house.

When Jesus goes into a house, it becomes a temple. When you go
into a temple, it becomes a house—because we carry our own temples inside. Wherever Jesus goes it becomes a temple, his presence
creates that sacred quality. And only when you bring the temple and
the freshness of the mountains, and the virginity of the mountains,
only then can you teach. You can teach only then, when you *have* it.

And early in the morning he came again into the temple, and all
    the people came unto him; and he sat down, and taught them.
And the scribes and Pharisees brought unto him a woman
    taken in adultery; and when they had set her in the midst,
They said unto him, Master, this woman was taken in
    adultery, in the very act.

Now Moses in the law commanded us, that such should be
stoned: but what sayest thou?

This is one of the most important parables in Jesus' life.
Go into it slowly, delicately, carefully.

And the scribes and Pharisees . . . Now for that you can read "the
moralists and the puritans." In those days, those were the names
of the moralists, the pundits, the scholars—the scribes and the
Pharisees. The Pharisees were the people who were very respectable. On their surfaces very moral, pretentious, with great
egos: "We are moral and everybody else is immoral"—and always
searching and looking into people's faults. Their whole life is
concerned with that: how to exaggerate their own qualities and
how to reduce others' qualities to nil.

The puritans, the moralists, *brought unto him a woman taken in
adultery.*

Now when you come to a man like Jesus, you have to come there
in humbleness, you have to come there to imbibe something from
Jesus; it is a rare opportunity. And now here come these fools and
they bring a woman. They bring their ordinary mind, their
mediocre mind, their stupidities with them.

And the scribes and Pharisees brought unto him a woman
taken in adultery . . .

They have not learned even this simple lesson that when
you go to a man like Jesus or Buddha, you go to partake, to participate in his consciousness: you go to become intimate with him.

You don't bring the ordinary problems of life there; they are irrelevant. That will be wasting a great opportunity; that will be wasting
Jesus' time. And he had not much time, as I told you before—only
three years of ministry. And these fools were wasting like this . . .
But they had a certain strategy in it: it was a trap.

They were not really concerned with the woman. They were
creating a trap for Jesus. It was a very cunning act.

And the scribes and Pharisees brought unto him a woman
taken in adultery; and when they had set her in the midst,
they said unto him, Master, this woman was taken in adultery,
in the very act.

Now what is adultery?

A conscious person will say if you don't love a man—maybe the
man is your own husband—if you don't love the man and you sleep
with the man, it is adultery. If you don't love the woman—and she
may be your own wife—if you don't love her and you sleep with her,
you are exploiting her, you are deceiving her. It is adultery.

But that is not the definition of the Pharisees and the puritans
and the scribes and the pundits. Their definition is legal, their
definition does not arise out of consciousness or love. Their definition arises out of the legal court. If the woman is not your wife
and you have been found sleeping with her, it is adultery. It is just
a legal matter, technical. The heart is not taken into account, only
the law. You may be deeply in love with the man or with the woman,
but that is not to be taken into account. The unconscious mind
cannot take higher things into account. He can only take the lowest into account.

His problem is always legal. Is it *your* woman? Your wife? Are you legally wed to her? Then it is good, then it is no longer sin. If she is not your woman, you are not legally wed to her . . . You may be in deep love, and you may have immense respect for the woman—you may almost be a worshipper of the woman—but it is sin, it is adultery.

These people brought this woman to Jesus, and . . .

They said unto him, Master, this woman was taken in
    adultery, in the very act.

Just the other day I was reading the memoirs of an English Christian missionary who went to Japan in the early days of this century. He was taken around Tokyo. His host took him around to show him the city. In one public bath there were men and women taking their baths in the nude. The missionary was very much shocked.

He stood there for five minutes, watched everything, and then he told his host, "Is it not immoral—women and men taking baths naked in a public place?"

And the host said, "Sir, this is not immoral in our country, but to stand here and watch is immoral. Sorry to say," he said, "but I am feeling very guilty standing with you, because that is *their* business if they want to take a bath naked. That is *their* freedom. But why are you standing here? This is ugly, immoral."

Now the missionary's standpoint is very ordinary, and the host's standpoint is extraordinary.

These people say, Master, this woman was taken in adultery, in the very act.

And what were *you* doing there? These were peeping Toms

or . . . what type of people were these? What were you doing there? Why should you be concerned? This woman's life is her life. How she wants to spend her life is her concern. Who are you to interfere? But the puritan, the moralist, has always been interfering in other people's lives. He is not democratic, he is very dictatorial. He wants to manipulate people, condemn people.

Now what were these people doing there?

And they say, *Master, this woman was taken in adultery, in the very act.*

They have caught the woman while she was making love.

One thing more: where is the man? She was doing adultery alone . . . ? Nobody has ever asked this question about this parable. I have read many Christian books, but nobody has ever asked, "Where is the man?"

But it is a man's society. It is always the woman who is wrong, not the man. The man will go free perfectly well. He may himself be a Pharisee, he may himself be a respectable man—but the woman has to be condemned. Have you not observed it? Prostitutes are condemned, but where are the prostituters? Where are those people? They may be the same people who condemn.

Puritans are always ugly people. They don't live, but then they don't allow anybody else to live. Their only joy is how to kill other people's joys, how to kill everybody's celebration.

Now what were these people doing there? Don't they have anything else to do? Don't they have their own women to love? What kind of people are these? They must be a little perverted to go out searching and seeking who is committing adultery. And then where is the man? Just the woman has to be condemned always.

Why does the woman have to be condemned? Because the woman is a woman and the man is the dominant one, and all the legal codes have been made by men. They are very prejudicial, biased. All the legal courts say what should be done to a woman if she is found in adultery, but they don't say anything about what should be done to the man. No, they say, "Boys are boys. And boys will be boys." It is always a question of the woman.

Even if a man rapes a woman, the woman becomes condemned; she loses respect, not the rapist!

This is an ugly state of affairs. This can't be called religious, it is very political—basically in man's favor and against woman. And all your so-called moralities have been that way.

In India, when a husband used to die, the wife had to go with him to the funeral pyre, then only was she thought to be virtuous. She had to become a *sati*, she had to die with the husband. If she did not die, that meant she was not virtuous. That simply meant she wanted to live without the husband, or maybe she wanted the husband to die, now she wanted freedom, now she would fall in love with somebody else.

In India it has been thought then that for the woman there is no life once the husband is dead. Her husband is her whole life. If the husband is gone, she has to go. But nothing is said about the man if his woman dies—no prescription for him that he should die with the woman. No, that is no problem. Immediately after the woman has died . . . In India it happens every day: the people are burning the woman, and then coming back home, they start thinking about the new marriage—where the man should find a new woman, how to find one. Not a single day is lost.

For man the morality is different, for woman it is different. Then it is a very unconscious morality, and a very *immoral* morality.

My definition of morality is that of consciousness, and consciousness is neither man nor woman. Consciousness is just consciousness. Only when something is decided by your being conscious will it be classless, will it be beyond the distinctions of body, caste, creed. And only then is it moral.

Master, they say, *this woman was taken in adultery, in the very act.*

Now Moses in the law commanded us, that such should be
stoned: but what sayest thou?
This they said, tempting him, that they might have to accuse
him. But Jesus stooped down, and with his finger wrote on the
ground, as though he heard them not.

This was the trap. They wanted to trap Jesus, because Moses
had said that such a woman should be stoned. Nothing is said
about the man. Such a woman should be stoned to death: Moses
has said this. Now they are creating a problem for Jesus. If Jesus
says, "Yes, do as Moses says," then they can accuse him, because
he has always been talking about love, compassion, kindness, forgiveness. Then they can say, "What about your compassion? What
about your forgiveness? What about your love? You say this woman
has to be killed by stones? This is hard and cruel and violent."
Tricky fellows.
And if Jesus says, "This is not right. Moses is not right," then
they can say, "So you have come to destroy Moses? So you have
come to destroy and corrupt our religion? And you have been saying to people, 'I have come not to destroy but to fulfill.' What
about that? If you have come to fulfill, then follow Moses' law!"
Now they are creating a dilemma. This is the trap. They are not
much concerned about the woman, remember, their real target is
Jesus; the woman is just an excuse. And they have brought such a
case . . . That's why they say *in the very act,* red-handed. So it is
not a question of deciding whether the woman has really committed adultery. Otherwise, Jesus will have an excuse to get out. He
will say, "First, try to find out whether *really* it has happened.
Bring the witnesses. Let it first be decided." Then it will take
years. So they say, "Red-handed! We have caught her in the very

act. We are all the witnesses, so there is no question of deciding anything else. And the law is clear: Moses has said that such should be stoned."

_____

. . . but what sayest thou?

_____

"Do you agree with Moses? If you agree, then what about your love and compassion—your whole message? If you don't agree, then what do you mean when you say, 'I have come to fulfill'? Then you have come to *destroy* Moses' law. So do you think you are higher than Moses? Do you think that you know more than Moses?"

_____

. . . but what sayest thou? This they said, tempting him, that they might have to accuse him. But Jesus stooped down, and with his finger wrote on the ground, as though he heard them not.

_____

Why? Why did Jesus stoop down? Why did he start writing on the ground?

They were just on the bank of a river. Jesus was sitting in the sand. Why has he started writing on the sand? What has happened?

There is one thing to be understood: it is always a delicate problem. For example, if I see something stated by Buddha as wrong, there is a great hesitation to say that he is wrong. He cannot be wrong. Tradition must have misinterpreted him. Something must have been wrongly put into his mouth. Buddha cannot be wrong. But now there is no way to decide, because the scriptures say this clearly . . .

Jesus hesitating . . . Jesus is concerned. He does not want to say a single word against Moses, but he has to say it, hence the hesitation. He does not want to say anything against Moses because Moses *cannot* say it that way. It is his inner feeling that Moses cannot say it that way. But the inner feeling cannot be decisive. These people will say, "Who are you? And why should we care about your inner feeling? We have the written code with us, given by our forefathers. It is there written clearly!"

Jesus does not want to say anything against Moses, because he *really* has come to fulfill Moses. Anybody who becomes enlightened in the world is always fulfilling all the enlightened ones that have preceded him. Even if sometimes he says something against them, then too he is fulfilling them, because he cannot say anything against them. And if you feel that he is saying something against them, then he is saying something against the tradition, against the scripture. But that looks like saying something against Moses, against Buddha, against Abraham. Hence, he stoops down. He starts looking at the sand and then starts writing. He is puzzled about what to do. He has to find a way out.

He has to find the way out in such a way that he has not to say anything against Moses, and yet he cancels the whole law. And he really comes with a very miraculous answer, a magical answer.

So when they continued asking him, he lifted up himself, and
said unto them, He that is without sin among you, let him
first cast a stone at her.

It is really incredible, it is beautiful—that was his hesitation. He has found a golden mean. He has not said a single word against Moses and he has not supported Moses either. This is the delicate point to understand.

Jesus was really utterly intelligent—uneducated, but utterly intelligent, a man of immense awareness. That's the only reason why he could find the way out.

He says, *He that is without sin among you* . . . He says, "Perfectly right"—does not say directly that Moses is right. But he says, "Perfectly right. If Moses says so, then it must be so. But then, who should start throwing stones at this woman?"

He that is without sin among you, let him first cast a stone
        at her.

"So start, but only those who are without sin . . ."

Now this is a new thing that Jesus brings in. You can judge only if you are without sin. You can punish only if you are without sin. If you are also in the same boat, then what is the point? Then who is going to punish whom?

And again he stooped down, and wrote on the ground.

Why did he stoop down again? Because he must have been afraid; some foolish person is always possible. He knows that everybody has committed one sin or other. If they have not com-

mitted, then they have been thinking to commit—which is almost
the same.

Whether you think or you act makes no difference. Remember,
the difference between sin and crime is this: crime has to be acted
out, only then is it crime. You can go on thinking, but if you don't
commit it to action, no court can punish you because it never becomes a crime. And only crime is within the jurisdiction of the court,
not sin. Then what is sin? Sin is if you think, I would like to murder
this man. No court can do anything. You can say, "Yes, I have been
thinking of it my whole life"—but thinking is beyond the court's jurisdiction. You are allowed to think. No court can punish you because
you dreamt that you killed somebody. You can dream every day, and
you can go on killing as many people as you want. No court can catch
hold of you unless it comes to actuality, unless thought becomes
deed, unless thought is translated into reality. If it comes out of you
and affects society, then it becomes crime. But it is sin, because God
can go on reading your thoughts. There is no need for him to read
your acts. The magistrate has to read your acts, he cannot read your
thoughts; he is not a thought-reader or a mind-reader.

But for God there is no difference; whether you think or you do,
it is all the same. The moment you think, you have done it.

So Jesus says, *He that is without sin among you* . . . not "without
crime." He says, *He that is without sin among you, let him first cast a
stone at her*. That distinction was known down the ages: that if you
think it, you have committed a sin already.

And again he stooped down . . .

Why this time? Because if he goes on looking at people, his very
look may be provocative. If he goes on looking at people then

somebody, just feeling offended by his look, may throw a stone at the poor woman. He does not want to offend; he withdraws. He simply stoops down, starts writing in the sand—again as if he is not there. He becomes absent, because his presence can be dangerous. If they have come just to trap him, and he is there and they feel his presence, it will be difficult for them to feel their own consciences, their own consciousnesses. He withdraws into himself, he allows them total freedom to think about it. He does not interfere; his look can be an interference.

He stoops down again, starts writing on the sand, gives them a chance—if they want to escape they can escape.

And they which heard it, being convicted by their own
   conscience . . .

Jesus leaves them alone. That is the beauty of the man. He does not even interfere by his presence; he is simply no more there. Their own consciences start pricking. They know. Maybe many times they have lusted after *this* woman, and maybe they themselves have been participants with this woman in the past. Maybe this woman is a prostitute, and all these respectable people in their turn have made love to her. Because one prostitute means that almost the whole town becomes involved.

In India, in the ancient days, prostitutes were called *nagarvadhu*, the wife of the town. That is the right name.

So all of these people must have been involved in some way or other with this woman or with other women—if not in acts, then in thoughts.

My feeling is it must be evening and the sun is setting, it is becoming dark and Jesus is writing on the sand, stooping down, and it becomes dark. And by and by people start disappearing in the dark.

> And they which heard it, being convicted by their own
> conscience, went out one by one, beginning at the
> eldest—the mayor—even unto the last . . .

First the eldest disappeared, because of course they have lived long, so they have sinned long. The young people may not be such great sinners; they have not had enough time yet. But the oldest disappeared first. Those who were standing in front, they must have moved slowly to the back, and then from the back they escaped. Because this man has really created a great problem: he has changed the whole situation. They had come to trap him and they are trapped.

You cannot trap a Jesus or a Buddha; it is impossible—you will be trapped. You exist at a lower state of mind. How can you trap a higher state of mind? That is just foolish. The higher state can trap you immediately, because from the higher state your whole being is available.

Now Jesus must have looked into these people's consciences— that was possible for him—he must have seen all kinds of sins raising their heads. In fact, even standing there, they were thinking about the woman: how to get hold of her. Maybe they were angry because somebody else had committed the sin and they were not given the opportunity. Maybe they were only jealous: maybe they wanted to be there instead of that man who had not been brought. Jesus must have looked from his height into their hearts. He has trapped them. They forget their trap completely, they forget about Moses and the law, et cetera. In fact, they were never worried about Moses and the law. This has also to be understood.

They were really more interested in stoning this woman, enjoying this murder. Not that they were interested in punishing somebody who had committed a sin; that was just an excuse. They could not leave this opportunity of murdering this woman. And now Moses can be used.

There are a thousand and one things said by Moses. They are not worried about them. They are not interested in all those sayings and all those statements. They are interested in this: that Moses says you can stone a woman if you catch hold of her in adultery. They can't miss this great opportunity of murder, of violence. And when violence can be committed according to the law, who would like to miss it? Not only will they enjoy the violence, they will enjoy that they are very, very legal people, virtuous followers of Moses. But they have all forgotten about it. Just a little turning by Jesus, and they have forgotten about Moses . . . He has changed the whole point. He has changed their minds from the woman to themselves. He has converted them, he has turned them backward—a one-hundred-eighty-degree turn. They were thinking about the woman and Moses and Jesus, and he has changed their whole attitude. He has made them their own target. He has turned their consciousness.

Now he says, "Look into yourself. If you have never committed a sin, then . . . then you are allowed, then you can kill this woman."

And Jesus was left alone, and the woman standing in the
    midst.
When Jesus had lifted up himself, and saw none but the
    woman, he said unto her, Woman, where are those thine
    accusers?

Now he is not saying, "I am accusing you." . . . *Where are those thine accusers?* He is not for a single moment a participant in it. He has not judged, he has not condemned. He has not said a single thing to the woman. He simply says:

Woman, where are those thine accusers? Hath no man
    condemned thee?

Have they all gone? Has no man thrown a stone at you?

She said, No man, lord.

She must have felt deep respect, reverence for this man, who has not only saved her physically, but who has not even accused her in any way. Spiritually also he has saved her. She must have looked into those eyes, which have only love and compassion and nothing else.

This is the religious man. The moralist is always condemning, accusing; the religious man, always accepting, forgiving.

She said, No man, lord. And Jesus said unto her, Neither do I
    condemn thee: Go, and sin no more.

Jesus says, "Nothing to be worried about—the past. The past is past, gone is gone. Forget about it. But take some lesson from this situation. Don't go on making the same mistakes in the future—if you think they are mistakes. I am not accusing you."

Neither do I condemn thee . . .

"But if you feel that you have done something wrong, then it is up to you. Don't do it again. Forget the past, and don't go on re-peating it."

That is the whole message of all the Buddhas and all the Christs and all the Krishnas: forget the past, and if you understand, then don't do it again. That's enough. There is no punishment, there is no judgment. If you have been doing something, you were help-less. You are unconscious, you have your limitations. You have your desires, unfulfilled desires. Whatsoever you have been doing was the only thing you could have done. So what is the point of ac-cusing and condemning you? The only thing that can be done is: your consciousness can be raised high.

And that woman must have moved into a high consciousness. She must have been afraid that she was going to be killed. Then this man, by a single statement, saved her from death. Not only that, those accusers disappeared. This man did a miracle! Not only did they not kill her, they simply became ashamed and escaped like thieves into the darkness of the night. This man is a magician.

And now, he is saying, "I don't condemn you. If you feel you have been doing something wrong, don't do it again. That's enough." He has converted the woman.

This is what acid people call a "contact high." Jesus is high. If you come into close affinity with him, you will start moving high. This is synchronicity—noncausal. The woman must have come there almost condemning herself, ashamed of herself, thinking to commit suicide. He has raised that woman, transformed that woman.

She said, No man, lord.

Jesus becomes Lord, Jesus becomes God to her. She has never seen such a godly man before. With no condemnation a man becomes a God. With no judgment a man becomes a God. And just his presence, a single statement, and those people disappeared and she is saved. And not only saved physically, but spiritually intact. Jesus has not interfered at all. He has not condemned, he has not said a single word. He simply says, "Don't repeat your past"— not a single word more. "Let the past be past and the gone, gone. You become new. All is good, and you are forgiven."

Jesus transformed many people by forgiving them. That was one of the accusations against him—that he forgives people. Who is he to forgive? Somebody has committed a sin—the society has to punish him! And if the society cannot punish and the man escapes, then the society has prepared a punishment through God— he should be thrown in hell.

Hindus also are very much against the idea that Jesus can forgive you. The Christian idea is immense, tremendous, very great and potential. Hindus say that you will have to suffer for your past karmas, whatsoever you have done, you will have to undo. If you have done a bad thing you will have to do a good thing. And the bad and its result are going to come: you will have to suffer the consequence. Hindus will not agree with this. Neither will the Buddhists agree, nor the Jains, nor were Jews agreeing with Jesus. How can he forgive?

But I say to you: a man of that understanding can forgive. Not that by his forgiving are you forgiven. But just if that consciousness, that great consciousness, can give you a feeling of well-being—"nothing is wrong, don't be worried; you can just shake off the past like dust and get out of it"—that very thing will give you such courage, such enthusiasm, will open new possibilities and new doors. And you are freed from it. You immediately move beyond it.

From this came the idea of Christian confession. It does not work that way, because the man you go to confess to is an ordinary man just like you. When you are confessing, the priest is not really forgiving you, he may be condemning deep down. His forgiveness is just a show. He is an ordinary man, he has no higher conscious-ness than you. Only from the higher can forgiveness flow. Only from the high mountains can the rivers flow toward the plains. Only from a Jesus or a Buddha can forgiveness flow. And when there is a man like Jesus or Buddha, just his touch, just his look, is enough to forgive you your whole past and all your *karmas*.

I totally agree with Jesus. He brings a new vision to humanity: to attain to freedom. The Hindu, the Jain, the Buddhist concept is very ordinary and mathematical. It has no magic in it. It is very logical but it has no love in it. Jesus brings love to the world.

Osho International
Meditation Resort

The Osho International Meditation Resort is a place where people can have a direct personal experience of a new way of living with more alertness, relaxation, and fun. Located about 100 miles southeast of Mumbai in Pune, India, the resort offers a variety of programs to thousands of people who visit each year from more than 100 countries around the world.

Originally developed as a summer retreat for Maharajas and wealthy British colonials, Pune is now a thriving modern city that is home to a number of universities and high-tech industries. The Meditation Resort spreads over forty acres in a tree-lined suburb known as Koregaon Park. The resort campus provides accommodation for a limited number of guests, and there is a plentiful variety of nearby hotels and private apartments available for stays of a few days up to several months.

Resort programs are all based in the Osho vision of a qualitatively new kind of human being who is able both to participate creatively in everyday life and to relax into silence and meditation. Most programs take place in modern, air-conditioned facilities and include a variety of individual sessions, courses, and workshops covering everything from creative arts to holistic health treatments, personal transformation and therapy, esoteric sciences, the Zen approach to sports and recreation, relationship issues, and significant life transitions for men and women. Individual sessions and group workshops are offered throughout the year, alongside a full daily schedule of meditations.

Outdoor cafes and restaurants within the resort grounds serve both traditional Indian fare and a choice of international dishes, all made with organically grown vegetables from the resort's own farm. The campus has its own private supply of safe, filtered water.

See www.osho.com/resort for more information, including travel tips, course schedules, and guesthouse bookings.

For More Information

about Osho and his work, see:
    www.osho.com
    a comprehensive Web site in several languages that includes an online tour of the Meditation Resort and a calendar of its course offerings, a catalog of books and tapes, a list of Osho information centers worldwide, and selections from Osho's talks.

    Or contact:
    Osho International
    e-mail: oshointernational@oshointernational.com

About the Author

Osho's teachings defy categorization, covering everything
from the individual quest for meaning to the most urgent social
and political issues facing society today. His books are not written
but are transcribed from audio and video recordings of extempo-
raneous talks given to international audiences over a period of
thirty-five years. Osho has been described by the London *Sunday
Times* as one of the "1000 Makers of the 20th Century" and by
American author Tom Robbins as "the most dangerous man since
Jesus Christ."

About his own work Osho has said that he is helping to create
the conditions for the birth of a new kind of human being. He has
often characterized this new human being as "Zorba the
Buddha"—capable both of enjoying the earthy pleasures of a Zorba

the Greek and the silent serenity of a Gautam Buddha. Running like a thread through all aspects of Osho's work is a vision that encompasses both the timeless wisdom of the East and the highest potential of Western science and technology.

Osho is also known for his revolutionary contribution to the science of inner transformation, with an approach to meditation that acknowledges the accelerated pace of contemporary life. His unique "Active Meditations" are designed to first release the accumulated stresses of body and mind, so that it is easier to experience the thought-free and relaxed state of meditation.

OSHO®

LOOK WITHIN...

BODY MIND BALANCING:
USING YOUR MIND TO HEAL YOUR BODY

Developed by Osho, BODY MIND BALANCING is a relaxation and meditation process for reconnecting with your body, complete with a guided audio process. The guided meditation and relaxation process, "Reminding Yourself of the Forgotten Language of Talking to Your BodyMind," accompanies the text on CD.

ISBN: 0-312-33444-3 • Paperback w/CD • $15.95/$17.95 Can.

MEDITATION:
A FIRST AND LAST FREEDOM

A practical guide to integrating meditation into all aspects of daily life, which includes instructions for over sixty meditation techniques, including the revolutionary Osho Active Meditations.™

ISBN: 0-312-33663-2 • Paperback • $13.95/$15.50 Can.

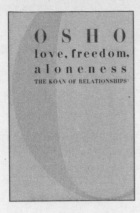

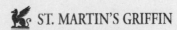

TAO: THE PATHLESS PATH

Contemporary interpretations of selected parables from the LIEH TZU reveal how the timeless wisdom of this 2500-year-old Taoist classic contains priceless insights for living today.

ISBN: 1-58063-225-4 • Paperback • $12.95/$14.50 Can.

ZEN: THE PATH OF PARADOX

"Zen is not a philosophy, it is poetry. It does not propose, it simply persuades. It does not argue, it simply sings its own song. It is aesthetic to the very core." In this book, Osho calls Zen "the path of paradox" and unfolds the paradox through delightful Zen anecdotes and riddles.

ISBN: 0-312-32049-3 • Paperback • $12.95/$14.50 Can.

YOGA: THE SCIENCE OF THE SOUL

Modern yoga emphasizes physical postures and exercises to increase flexibility and aid in relaxation. But yoga has its roots in the understanding of human consciousness and its potential. Explore this potential with Osho's unique insights into yoga and its relationship to the modern mind.

ISBN: 0-312-30614-8 • Paperback • $13.95/$16.95 Can.

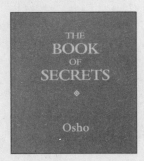
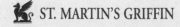

The Man Who Loved Seagulls

More Osho Books